No Greater Story

Rediscovering your place in God's epic adventure

Leon Evans

malcolm down
PUBLISHING

British Library Cataloguing in Publication Data

A catalogue record for this book is available from the
British Library.

ISBN 978-1-917455-12-1

Cover design by Mark Steel
Art direction by Sarah Grace

Printed and bound in the UK by Short Run Press Ltd, Exeter

Typset in the Grace Typeface

The Grace Typeface has been developed over many years in partnership with Sarah Grace, 2K Denmark and Cambridge University. This ground-breaking typeface aims to improve readability and reduce visual stress for people with dyslexia and other reading difficulties.

What others are saying . . .

This extraordinary book helps us all understand the greatness of God and the greatness of his story. Accessible, inspirational and a resource for every church and Christian to understand our part in the No Greater Story.

Rev. Dr Cris Rogers
Rector of All Hallows Bow and Chair of the Spring Harvest
planning group

This book leaves me feeling hopeful. In recent years we have all experienced what Leon describes as 'an unprecedented era of chaos, crisis and calamity at a global level', but we can take courage in the knowledge that God is still in control and fulfilling his promises on the earth. This book calls you and me to be part of that redemptive story.

Debra Green OBE, DL
Founder of Redeeming Our Communities

There can be no deeper privilege than being a child of God, and in his book, Leon reminds us that there is no greater story than the great story of God. He invites us to find our place in the purposes and plans of God. His words are magnetic, and draw us towards the heart of God. His words pack a punch as he unpacks this great theme. By weaving biblical reflection, personal application and living examples, he weaves a tapestry of invitation into the greatest and most exciting endeavour in human history – the call to find our identity in Christ, see what God is doing in the world, join the Holy Spirit in the redemption story. Buy the book, read it and apply it. A resource for individuals, small groups and churches. I pray it will bless, strengthen and inspire you.

Rev. Malcolm Duncan, FRSA, FIPT
Senior minister, KTLCC

In a seamless flow, this book tells God's story and weaves into it yours and mine as well. Deep truths of Scripture are laid out so clearly and plainly that your mind is enlightened, your heart stirred and you end up with a fresh appreciation of Jesus and all he has done for us.

Paul Reid
Pastor emeritus, CFC, Belfast

Isaiah can be an intimidating book to navigate! Yet Leon theologically, sensitively and pastorally unpacks God's story, offering profound insights and encouragement for modern-day Christians. His inimitable narrative guides us through Isaiah's key themes and timeless truths, propelling us towards a maturing faith that reflects God's love, justice and faithfulness.

Olivia Amartey
Executive director, Elim Pentecostal Church UK and NI

Accessible, authentic and practical, Leon not only calls us afresh to the greatest story, but he writes as a seasoned pastor, a practical theologian – and does all this with the heart and tone of a friend. Don't miss this.

Jeff Lucas
Author, speaker, broadcaster

Whatever your own story, you will find perspective, purpose and hope in the pages of this book. Leon weaves together biblical insight, personal testimony and practical application in a way that will inspire and equip individuals, small groups and churches to engage with God's redemptive story. Highly recommended!

Cathy Madavan
Speaker, author and member of the Spring Harvest planning group

Accessible, biblical, challenging and encouraging. This book is a wonderful gift to the church at this key cultural moment.

Gavin Calver
CEO, Evangelical Alliance

Contents

The Living Room

The Playground

PART THREE: Perfecter

The Classroom

The Living Room

The Playground

Dedication and Thanks

I want to dedicate this book to my incredible church family, Lifecentral Church. For more than thirty years, we have had the joy and privilege of helping lead you; you are one of the most amazing church communities I know. Your constant passion to reach people, your willingness to change, your love for Jesus and our community is telling a story of creativity and redemption, and much of the inspiration for this book comes from you – thank you!

There are so many other people I want to thank: the Spring Harvest planning group and team for your constant encouragement and feedback; you model kingdom culture and team. For all of those who generously submitted ideas and resources to be included in this book – Care for the Family, Compassion UK, Home For Good, A Rocha UK, 24:7, Further Faster Network, Faith in Later Life, Alpha UK, Ruth Valerio, Mark Greenwood – thank you.

For my friends Tom Gregory (spoken word poem), Mark Welch, Pete Hopper (artwork), Russ Sargeant (illustration) for your creative pieces which add colour to the words on the pages – thank you.

To my many friends and mentors who over the years have helped shape me, because our story is not a solitary pursuit but a community endeavour. You have helped me find my place in God's greater story, especially when at times it was not the story I wanted – thank you.

To Helen and Mark Robertson for allowing me to sit in your 'garden shed' for many weeks as I tried to write, often finding myself staring at empty pages – thank you.

To my family, those alive and those in heaven: you have modelled what it means to live the story, you have invested in me and cheered me on and I am grateful we get to be a part of the story together – thank you.

Finally, to my wife and best friend, Allison. Our story together began many years ago as teenagers and over the years you have constantly encouraged me, inspired me and made me better – thank you.

A Helpful User Guide

How to get the best out of
No Greater Story

Every great story has a beginning, a middle and an end, the story of God is no exception. To help you get the most out of this resource (which I hope is much more than a book), let me explain how the journey will work.

No Greater Story is split into three parts, and within each part there are three different environments for us to discover, grow and learn.

The Classroom – this is the place for INFORMATION. This is where we will dive into theology primarily through the book of Isaiah as we explore the greater story of God. For some of us newer to faith or exploring faith, there may be brand-new information here; for others, it will be a reminder of what we already know but may have forgotten.

The Living Room – this is the place where we get to see how what we've learned in the classroom plays out in the living room of life. What does it mean that God is GREATER than anything we can encounter in our own story? My hope and desire for you is that you will find INSPIRATION that will be added to the INFORMATION you learn in the classroom.

The Playground – this is the place where we get to take the INFORMATION we've learned mixed with the INSPIRATION, and live it out. This is where APPLICATION takes centre stage. The Playground is where we all get to 'play' in the greater story of God. The epic adventure God invites us into is not reserved for the few, the theologically trained or for the elite, but for anyone who responds to the invitation to follow Jesus into the greater story God is writing for planet Earth. The Playground also has three levels: *my life, my home, my church.* There are activities to do on your own and with others there are also resources to access and ideas to 'play' with. The resources are accessible via the QR code which will take you to a website full of creative ideas and activities.

As we put these three things together, what are we aiming for at the end?

INFORMATION + INSPIRATION + APPLICATION = TRANSFORMATION

> And we all, with unveiled face, *continually* seeing as in a mirror the glory of the Lord, are *progressively* being transformed into His image from [one degree of] glory to [even more] glory, which comes from the Lord, [who is] the Spirit.'
> (2 Corinthians 3:18, AMP)

Let the story begin . . .

Prologue

Our younger son, Simeon, had no fear of animals whatsoever. Now, at times this was a little scary as he would often go face to face with fierce-looking dogs, and even once tried to get out of the car to stroke the big 'cat' which was actually a lion in the safari park! (I haven't told my wife this story so let's keep it between us!) You see, our son Simeon has complex additional needs and learning disabilities, and when he was younger had zero fear of animals. That was until one day at a farm when he spotted in the distance a horse, and ran towards it. As he approached, he suddenly began to realise this was a bigger horse than he'd ever seen – it was a Shire horse and it was huge, so much greater than any animal he had encountered before.

All of a sudden, Simeon stopped. Fear gripped him and instinctively he lifted his arms up towards me as if to say, 'Daddy, lift me up.' I immediately swooped in and put him on my shoulders and in an instant, his fear disappeared and calm returned once more.

At that moment I sensed God say, 'Everything looks different when you're on Daddy's shoulders.'

Perspective is everything

If the theologian and author A.W. Tozer was correct when he famously said, 'What comes into our minds when we think about God is the most important thing about us',[1] then I'd suggest many of us have a perspective issue right now. For some of us, our view of God has often been shaped by our life experiences, hurts and disappointments. In the 1950s, J.B. Phillips wrote a book entitled *Your God is Too Small*[2] and then in the 1980s, John Young wrote a book entitled, *Our God is Still Too Small*,[3] suggesting this perspective problem is an ongoing issue we face in every generation. Decades later, is it possible that our view of God has been diminished even further?

We have all endured an unprecedented era of chaos, crisis and calamity at a global level, a church level and for many of us, a personal level. It's left us exhausted, confused, uncertain, fearful and wondering if God is still in control or able to fulfil his purposes on the earth.

It's easy at times like these to identify with the children of Israel in the Old Testament who on leaving Egypt, found themselves exploring the promised land but were confronted by giants, their 'Shire horses', if you will, and their response was to cry out, 'We seemed like grasshoppers in our own eyes' (Numbers 13:33).

What they needed was to metaphorically jump on 'Daddy's' shoulders to find a better perspective, to gain a bigger view of God and in doing so, see the greater story that God was inviting them into. The good news is that today we can do exactly the same.

To help us we need a storyteller, a time-travelling narrator who can help us rediscover this greater story again, but before we get to the story, let's see where we are starting from . . .

Introduction

We all have a story, and our story matters. If we are honest, nobody gets the story they really want, but here's the amazing truth: everybody's story can find meaning and purpose when it's part of a bigger story … a greater story.

In order to locate our story and see it as part of a greater story, we need first to establish where we are. Have you ever been to a theme park and you're desperate to get to that special ride you've heard so much about, so you head to the site map, and what do you search for? Not for the ride you're so excited to experience, but for the words 'you are here'.

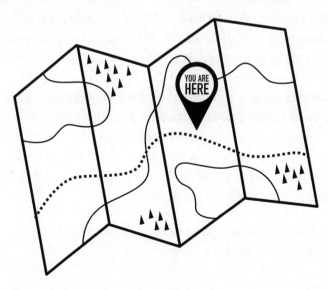

If you don't know where you are, it's hard to get to where you want to go

Many historians, sociologists and social commentators believe we are living in what's been termed a 'grey zone'; a space between one age and the next. An era where the way we see the world and the way we engage with that world is changing at a rapid rate. Pope Francis said, 'We are not living in an era of change but a change of era.'[4] We all see the rapid rate of change all around us, and at times it can feel hard to keep up, but in many senses we are living in something beyond what we have all experienced in our lifetimes. The explosion of technology, globalisation and political instability all point towards an era of seismic shift akin to what the world experienced moving from the agricultural age to the industrial age. One of the words used to describe this grey zone is 'permacrisis', which is a period of time marked by crisis after crisis with no end in sight.

This seems such an apt description of what we've experienced in recent years, geo-political turmoil, a global pandemic, cost of living crisis, confusion around human sexuality, culture wars, race wars and, of course . . . far too many actual wars. With this state of permacrisis comes a collapse of certainty, and sadly one of the impacts of that is that it can lead to increases in anxiety and mental health challenges. According to the World Health Organization, in 2019 there were 970 million people around the world living with a mental disorder, with anxiety and depression being the most common. Initial estimates suggested these numbers rose by almost 30 per cent because of the COVID-19 pandemic.[5]

Then there's the Church, and the picture, certainly in the Western world, is far from rosy.

We have seen alarming trends and trajectories that seem to scream at us 'decline', as we see historical denominations reporting falling attendances and closure of church buildings. This is compounded by leaders reporting increased levels of burnout and, of course, the many disturbing scandals, all of which add to the apparent collapse of certainty. According to Barna research, record numbers of Church leaders, certainly in the Western world, are considering quitting the full-time ministry, with some estimating as many as 42 per cent in March 2022.[6]

It's into this arena that we need to rediscover a story . . . *a greater story.*

Stories are powerful; they draw us in, they inspire us, we identify and see our place within that story. They give us what we all deep down aspire to, that sense of identity, meaning and purpose, a context to make sense of our life lived within that big story. Another name for the big story is the meta narrative. Meta is from the Greek word which means 'beyond or after' and suggests something transcending or overarching. In recent years we've seen the collapse of many of the meta narratives; many of the 'big' stories have lost their appeal and, in some cases, seem to be nothing more than history rather than lived out reality.

In 2009 the New Atheism movement seemed to be riding the peak of its wave with the assertion that belief in God was dead. Following on from books such as *God is Not Great* by Christopher Hitchens[7] and *The God Delusion* by Richard Dawkins,[8] this wave came to a head most notably with the campaign in 2008 funded by the British Humanist Society where buses in London carried the message, 'There's probably no god. Now stop worrying and enjoy your life.'[9]

The word 'probably' in that statement always makes me smile. I mean, why insert that word 'probably'? Apparently it was for scientific reasons as you can't empirically or scientifically prove there is no God!

We have also seen a rise in the suggestion that metanarratives are a thing of the past. The postmodern view is that any type of big, overarching story that we can universally connect our story into is outdated. The assertion is we are now beyond that type of objective truth and that anything that tries to provide any sense of cohesion, order or universal meaning must be false and something to be rejected at all costs. In truth, we are moving beyond postmodernism to what's being called metamodernism, which at its core embraces ambiguity, reconstruction and paradox. The demise of the big stories, I believe, has resulted in greater polarisation, greater loss of cohesiveness and a greater sense of fragmentation. The reality is you can reject the idea of the God story, but what do you replace it with in terms of its role and function in our lives? We end up living in a world of almost cosmic plagiarism, where we live off the borrowed blessings of Christianity but fail to acknowledge the source of those blessings. In many ways our culture has lost any sense of the 'why' to life.

With the collapse of the big stories has come the rise of the self, the idea being 'You do you . . . be yourself . . . find your truth . . . you are enough' but the problem with these kinds of assertions is that they aren't actually true. When we only place self at the centre of our story we lose the identity, meaning and purpose we crave for and were created for. I want to suggest some of this type of narrative has affected Christians as it's become not only our ideology but maybe also our theology. I once heard a preacher humorously ask his audience, 'What's the difference between a cat and a dog?' He then answered, 'A dog thinks, "You love me, you pat me you feed me, you must be god." A cat thinks, "You love me, you pat me, you feed me, I must be god!"'[10] We have become much more like cats than dogs in so many ways. The problem is, when you place self in the centre of the story, your view of God can result in someone just a little bit bigger and better than you, and he is far beyond that; he is so much greater.

Something remarkable took place in the UK in 2022 that had ripples all around the globe. On 8 September 2022 Queen Elizabeth II died at Balmoral Castle in Scotland, and more than 250,000 people went to visit her body as she lay in state at Westminster Hall, London. What we witnessed will never be forgotten by many of us; the range of people there, young and old, black and white, those with faith and those with none. Yet in that mixed crowd there was a unifying reverence, a uniting sense of awe. My pondering was over this question, 'What prompted people to make the sign of the cross, the bows, the nods, the tears?' Surely it was more than nostalgia, tradition or emotion? Could it be that the Queen provided a sense of transcendence, of otherness, of a life beyond, of a story that was 'greater' that somehow gave our lives that sense of meaning, identity and purpose? With all of our technological and cultural 'advancement', there's something deep within us that yearns for the big story, that longs for something overarching, something 'beyond', and as much as we try to resist, it keeps tugging at our hearts and minds, calling us to an adventure that is worthy, and dare I even say . . . epic.

We need to rediscover a big story once again, and to help us with that we need a storyteller . . . enter stage left . . . Isaiah.

The book of Isaiah is a titan of Scripture, a colossus of a book and, in places, quite a conundrum for theologians and scholars. It's been likened to Romans in the New Testament in terms of its complexity, importance and the vast sweep of its message. It's almost a microcosm of the Bible as it contains sixty-six chapters mirroring the sixty-six books of the Bible. It's a book that, while set in a time and place in history, speaks to a specific people group; it is also a book that tells the greater story of God. Like any great story, the story of God has a beginning, a middle and end that we will explore together as we go on this journey. This story could be summarised by these 'mountain peaks':

CREATION

FALL

REDEMPTION

PERFECTION

Creation – Fall – Redemption – Perfection

In the creation section we will look at how Isaiah points us to the beginning of the story, the origin, if you like, with God as the Creator and initiator of his story. The Fall and redemption are interlinked; we will look at how sin and disobedience disrupted the story, and how God was in the same story, launching his plan of redemption through a Messiah (Jesus). Isaiah sees this beautifully and powerfully, not only in the world around him but forward prophetically to what God will do in restoring humanity back to God. Finally, we will look through Isaiah's eyes as he sees way into the future when all things will be made new; the new heavens and the new earth, the completion or the word we will use, the perfection. Isaiah sees the broad sweep of the greater story of God and all the time God is inviting us, as he invited Isaiah, to rediscover our part in this epic adventure story.

What do we know?

The book covers a period of history that spans approximately 200 years and four kings between the latter half of the eighth to the latter half of the sixth centuries BC. It begins with the prophet addressing the situation before him where he sees a people displaced from their homeland, a people who have turned away from their God and forgotten what it means to be the people of God. There then comes a moment of crisis that becomes a catalyst for Isaiah and for the story. This moment happened in the year King Uzziah died so we know that's 740 BC. Uzziah was mostly a good king who ruled the southern kingdom of Judah, which had enjoyed a period of peace and prosperity, but times were changing. The people of God were turning away from God, the divide between the rich and poor was growing and the surrounding kingdoms were bearing down on Judah, especially the kingdom of Assyria (now northern Iraq and southern Turkey).

King Uzziah, who began so well, failed to finish well, as recorded in other parts of the Old Testament: 'But after Uzziah became powerful, his pride led to his downfall. He was unfaithful to the LORD his God . . .' (2 Chronicles 26:16).

This is also reflected in the people; as their wealth increased, so did their faithlessness to God. As they gained more 'stuff', their spiritual hunger and reliance on God began to diminish.

I saw a powerful demonstration of this in Bulgaria in the 1990s just after communism collapsed. As this harsh and oppressive regime that made faith so difficult to live out ended, so a spiritual hunger in that nation was renewed as people threw off the constraints of a totalitarian government and hungered again for the greater story of God. We saw hundreds if not thousands of people come to faith on the streets in the early to mid-1990s, but then it soon began to change. As 'freedom' started to gain traction so options and opportunities started to materialise. As people gained more in terms of money and wealth, their hunger for God and his story began to wane.

It's an all too familiar pattern . . . it's an all too human story

King Uzziah contracted leprosy and so became alienated physically, socially and spiritually; eventually his son Jotham succeeded him. The new king, Jotham, was generally a good king but he was followed by Ahaz, who made several alliances with other kingdoms that resulted in periods of great instability for the tribe of Judah. Then Hezekiah came to the throne, and it was he who ushered in a new season for the nation, including many reforms, and the story began to change – although never quite to the degree the people hoped for or expected.

What are we unsure about?

Who actually wrote it! The authorship of the book of Isaiah is a hotly contested debate, and this debate centres on whether there is one Isaiah, multiple Isaiahs or even multiple authors.

The theory of multiple Isaiahs originally proposed by Bernard Duhm in the nineteenth century divides the book into three: Proto Isaiah (1-39), Deutro Isaiah (40-55), Trito Isaiah (56-66).[11]

The view that Isaiah was written not by one Isaiah but either many Isaiahs or many different authors is due to several factors: the length of time the book spans, the differing writing styles in evidence, problems with certain events and characters of history, and whether, if it was a single writer, they could have known those facts and details. One of the key issues is the prophetic words thought to connect to the future arrival on the scene of King Cyrus (Isaiah 41:25) who is instrumental in the return from exile of the Jews back to their homeland. We know from history this occurs some 200 years after the time of Isaiah, so how could one Isaiah have written this? I will leave the nuances of this debate to scholars but needless to say, I don't think it really matters! We can be certain God inspired the writing of Isaiah, as he did for the whole of the Bible.

What can we be absolutely sure about?

Whether there was one Isaiah, more than one Isaiah, or multiple authors, the book of Isaiah possesses a unity and an authority that is unquestionable. Its primary value is its message, and in many ways it is a microcosm of the entirety of the Bible which, while written by multiple writers across hundreds of years with differing styles, still manages to retain a unity of message and story. Even if it were several writers, or, as some assert, Isaiah and his school of disciples who also contributed to the writing, there is still such a unity of message. Many writers with one 'editor in chief' can produce a work of startling unity, and that's what we have in the book of Isaiah.

With this in mind, we will refer to Isaiah in the singular form as if one person; he is our storyteller, our time-travelling narrator; he is the one who will help us sit where we need to sit so we can see what we need to see; he is the one who will help us gain a bigger view of God, and he is the one who will invite us into this story.

So, let's begin with what was to be for Isaiah the defining moment in his story.

Isaiah's AHA Moment

It was happening right in front of his eyes – the demise and disintegration of all he had held valuable, and he felt totally powerless to do anything about it. Isaiah was watching not only his nation turn away from God, not only the growing threat of the neighbouring superpower, Assyria, bearing down on Judah, but maybe saddest of all, his once great leader, mentor and friend King Uzziah becoming a shadow of his former self. A reign that had begun so well was fading away fast. Complacency and pride had gripped the king and subsequently that affected the whole nation. It was as if the big story Isaiah had known was now coming to an end.

Somewhere in the final year of the king's life, Isaiah had his awakening moment, a moment of such startling clarity that everything in his life and outlook changed. It was almost like he had been looking at life as a black and white TV and now it was not only glorious Technicolor but full HD with DolbyX surround sound!

We read in Isaiah 6 these life-changing words: 'In the year that King Uzziah died, I saw the Lord' (Isaiah 6:1a).

As his earthly king was dying, he saw his heavenly King who was very much alive

This experience Isaiah records changed everything for him, and it's an experience that can do the same for us. In his excellent book, *AHA*, Kyle Idleman talks about spiritual transformation and suggests that we all need to have that AHA moment that he defines as 'awakening – honesty – action'.[12] In the book he gives even more definition for this process by using these phrases: 'A sudden *awakening* – Brutal *honesty* – Immediate *action*'.

All three stages are vital if we are to not only be the people God wants us to be, but also play our part in the epic adventure story God is writing in the earth. You can observe similar experiences and stages for almost every character in the Bible who each had their own AHA moments.

Moses at the burning bush (Exodus 3), Gideon in the wine press (Judges 6), Mary as the angel visited her with life-altering news (Luke 1), Peter in his boat as Jesus calls him to the greater story of fishing for people not just for perch (Luke 5), the prodigal son returning home to the Father (Luke 15).

The ancient Church fathers and mothers used similar language to describe the cycle and process of spiritual transformation: 'Awakening – Purgation – Illumination – Union'.[13]

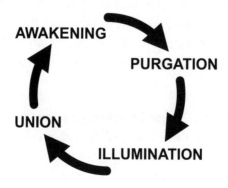

This is the process Isaiah went through, and it's the one God invites you and me to embark on as we embrace his *greater story*. For Isaiah, this journey of awakening, honesty and action consisted of three revelations about God and himself; each revelation takes you a stage further:

Stage 1: Divine holiness

> In the year that King Uzziah died, I saw the Lord, high and exalted, seated on a throne; and the train of his robe filled the temple.
>
> (Isaiah 6:1)

Notice Isaiah says he sees 'the Lord' and uses the name for God 'Adonai' meaning *absolute, ultimate, supreme*, the idea here is to convey the rulership and majesty of God.

Everything about this encounter speaks of royalty; even when an earthly monarch is seated, they are always higher positionally than anyone else, and that means something significant as it clarifies where power and authority resides. At the centre of this vision is the holiness of God, and the word 'holy' is used more times in the book of Isaiah than in the rest of the Old Testament put together!

The holiness of God is the only thing capable of filling the whole earth with glory. How it is that Isaiah is enabled to see the Lord we don't really know; it's a mystery, as God is spirit and several times in Scripture the seeing of God is prohibited (Exodus 33:20; 1 Timothy 6:16; 1 John 4:12). Yet in his graciousness God allows Isaiah a ringside seat to view his majesty and divine holiness, and it's quite an event! In trying to scramble for words, images, metaphors to help give us a window into the heavenly world Isaiah experienced, my mind raced back in time to some historical events.

For those of you old enough to remember the wedding of Prince Charles and Lady Diana in 1981, there's one image I can still recall, and that's the vastness of the train of Diana's dress. The scene was captured on camera by a panoramic shot and it was truly magnificent, measuring 25ft. It didn't exactly 'fill the temple' but it was impressive. Even though for many watching it was a showstopper, it didn't come even close to what Isaiah experienced.

Then my mind went back to the old USSR (now Russia) when it was at its military peak. I had the privilege of visiting Moscow in 1990, the year after the collapse of the Berlin Wall. In those days the body of Lenin was still in the mausoleum in Red Square, and I still remember the pomp and grandeur that regime displayed. In fact, prior to 1989, every 1 May was designated International Workers' Day; the military paraded its power and might. The goose-stepping soldiers, the array of tanks and military hardware were all showcased in order to evoke awe, grandeur and maybe just a little terror. None of this came even close to what Isaiah saw, heard and felt.

What Isaiah sees was way beyond anything we have ever seen; it was a heavenly parade of majesty, might and glory and it takes his breath away. He sees seraphim, which are angelic beings, some covering their feet and some their faces. Why did they cover their feet?

Some commentators suggest it's a reference to hiding parts they'd be embarrassed to be on show; others suggest the seraphim are symbolically disavowing the intention to go their own direction and instead demonstrating that they exist to do the bidding of their God.

Isaiah doesn't just see incredible things, he then hears incredible voices, angelic voices which he describes this way:

And they were calling to one another: 'Holy, holy, holy is the LORD Almighty; the whole earth is full of his glory.' At the sound of their voices the doorposts and thresholds shook and the temple was filled with smoke.

(Isaiah 6:3-4)

On a trip to Israel a few years ago, we had the privilege of leading a group of around 120 people, and on our Jerusalem day we went into the Church of St Anne by the pool of Bethesda. There I led our group in an acapella version of the song 'Agnus Dei' which centres around the word 'holy'.

The acoustics are so incredible I will never forget the sound we made in that space; the reverberation, the resonance, the richness was truly unforgettable; it was almost angelic voices – well, *almost*. Yet what Isaiah experienced was far greater than anything we have ever heard on earth.

Why in Isaiah 6 is the word 'holy' used three times, and in other places in the Bible?

This reminds me of when I was a worship leader and someone tried to use this verse to argue the point we should not repeat songs more than three times, because the Bible says 'holy, holy, holy'! Actually, this literary tool of repetition is often used in the Bible to make emphasis. There is no word in Hebrew for 'very' so repeating the words implies growing emphasis each time the word is used. The sense of greatness grows with each repeating word, so it could read, 'holy, holier, holiest'.

Within these words there's a challenge for Isaiah and certainly for us. 'The whole earth is full of his glory' is what the seraphim declared, but what if that's not our current experience or reality? As Isaiah looked around his world, there was not a lot of glory on show. Would he agree the whole earth was full of God's glory? I'm not convinced he would. As we look around our world, our Church or our own lives, do we see the glory of God in evidence? Would we agree the whole earth is full of God's glory? This raises a question we all need to learn how to grapple with, and it's this: 'If God is good, surely he can't be great, and if God is great, surely he can't be good?'

This question raises a tension we will wrestle with throughout this book as we explore this theme of 'no greater story' because as I often say: 'Some of what I see in life makes little sense, but without God it makes no sense at all.'

The vision Isaiah is given is one that transcends what he sees in the mere temporal or earthly realm. God is great and the whole earth is filled with his glory because he created it and he is still at work within that creation, we just don't see the fullness yet.

Isaiah sees the Lord; the word used for 'see' is the Hebrew word *raah,* which means, 'to look at, to inspect, to perceive, to consider, to behold'. I want to suggest it's much more of a gaze than a glance. I do wonder in my own life if I've lost the ability to gaze at God. Life is so busy, there are so many distractions, voices and screens vying for our attention that maybe we give God a cursory glance now and then rather than a fixed gaze. Over time, does that reduce our awareness of just how vast, great and holy our God really is? As Isaiah gazes on the majesty of God he sees something, he hears something, he feels something, he even smells something, and as all of his senses are awakened, something profound stirs within him, which propels him to the next revelation, to the next stage of his AHA moment.

Stage 2: Human sinfulness

Isaiah launches into the use of one of his favourite words – 'woe'. In fact, in the previous chapter lots of people receive a tirade of his woes!

Woe to you who add house to house and join field to
field till no space is left and you live alone in the land . . .
Woe to those who rise early in the morning to run after
their drinks . . . Woe to those who call evil good and
good evil . . . Woe to those who are wise in their own
eyes and clever in their own sight.

(Isaiah 5:8,11,20-21)

Woe is commonly understood to mean a great sadness and
have you noticed how easy it is to spot what makes us sad in
others but not in ourselves? Isn't it true that what others say
or do makes perfect sense to them, but rarely makes perfect
sense to us? We often judge others based on their actions, but
judge ourselves based on our intentions. Isaiah had a gift for
spotting woe in others, but here it changes as the vision of
God's divine majesty leads to an awakening that leads to brutal
honesty: "'Woe to me!' I cried. "I am ruined! For I am a man of
unclean lips, and I live among a people of unclean lips, and my
eyes have seen the King, the LORD Almighty'" (Isaiah 6:5).

Woe to you becomes woe to me.

There is a famous story of the writer G.K. Chesterton who
responded to a question posed in *The Times* newspaper that
simply asked, 'What is wrong with the world today?' If that
question was asked today, I guarantee most of us would
have an answer that revolved around other people being the
cause of the fault with the world! G.K. Chesterton's response,
however, was different; his response was both brief and
brilliant as he wrote:

Dear Sir,

I AM.

Yours,

G.K. Chesterton.[14]

Isaiah also makes this profound shift by the admission of his own brokenness and sin, and he uses the word 'ruined'; other translations say 'undone', 'lost', 'doomed'. All these words accurately portray the essence of what was happening to Isaiah, as his sense of self in comparison to a holy majestic God was beginning to grip his soul. He then seems to confess what is the cause of him feeling undone, lost, doomed and it's to do with what he calls his 'unclean lips'. It is a strange assertion by Isaiah, as he was known for his skill with words; after all, the poetry and oratory in his book are among some of the finest not only in the Bible but in all literature. So, what does he mean by 'unclean lips'? We can't be certain but maybe we could hazard some guesses:

> Could it be that over time the words of others who didn't profess to follow God became the words he allowed on his own lips?

> Could it be that under the pressure of the changing culture, Isaiah allowed his words to be affected, even corrupted by the very people he was trying to influence?

> Could it be that out of a desire to fit in or not to miss out, he allowed his words to lose their salt, to lose their light and ultimately to lose their power?

Could it be that his story is also our story?

If we are brutally honest, how many of us would say 'woe to me' at this point?

Have we allowed our words to be affected by the words we hear around us? Have we allowed the words on our lips to lose their power and potency? Have we allowed the culture we've been trying to influence actually influence us? As I sit in a coffee shop and write these words, our nation is in the grip of riots on our streets marked by division and polarisation almost greater than at any time I can remember. As followers of Jesus, are our words being shaped more by social media, or by the rhetoric that breeds hate and division, rather than by the Bible and by the greater story of God?

The reality for us all is that sometimes our lips betray the condition of our hearts. The Bible frequently draws a line of connection between what we say and the state of our hearts: 'For the mouth speaks what the heart is full of.' (NIV)

If we are brutally honest, sometimes our words do reveal the condition of our heart. Not just the words we speak out loud, but also the words we speak to ourselves. Not just the obviously 'unclean' words but the words of despair and defeat, 'Nothing will ever change, this is as good as it gets, God will never use me' and the list goes on and on.

Yet Isaiah didn't stay in his woes; there was another revelation to come, another AHA moment.

Stage 3: Gracious forgiveness

> Then one of the seraphim flew to me with a live coal in his hand, which he had taken with tongs from the altar. With it he touched my mouth and said, 'See, this has touched your lips; your guilt is taken away and your sin atoned for.'
>
> (Isaiah 6:6-7)

Please note that Isaiah did nothing in this moment other than receive. The verbs used here for 'touched' and 'atoned for' are in the coordinate perfect tense, which means that when one happened the other happened instantly and at the same time. When Isaiah is brutally honest with himself and God, he can then receive the gracious forgiveness of God, then his guilt and sin are removed. We are not sure what specific altar is in question here, the one before the veil or the bronze altar in the inner court, but it doesn't really matter. What matters is that Isaiah was receiving something from an altar. The history of Israel that Isaiah and other prophets constantly had to address was the way the people of God allowed the altars to be destroyed, damaged, neglected, abandoned or replaced by false gods. Can I suggest, *nothing will alter without an altar.*

Isaiah is not cleansed by his own effort, but by the grace of God that flows from the altar of God. With it there seems to rise within Isaiah a desire to consecrate himself to God and to God's story. The call to a life of goodness, meaning and purpose that reflects the holiness of God is not an austere proposition but a beautiful invitation to something better, something greater. What Isaiah realised in his AHA moment was that God always has more for us if we would only surrender to his will and to his call. What's more, this opens the way for something else as he now hears the voice of God speak:

> Then I heard the voice of the Lord saying, 'Whom shall I send? And who will go for us?' And I said, 'Here am I. Send me!'
>
> (Isaiah 6:8)

We often want to hear the voice of God and with it the call and plan of God, but until we've travelled this journey as Isaiah did through *awakening* into *honesty*, I'm not sure we are ready for the *action* God has for us. Now Isaiah is ready, his AHA moment has given him a greater vision of God, a deeper awareness of his own sinfulness, a more profound experience of gracious forgiveness which culminates in a willingness to serve the Lord whatever the cost. Note something really important here and it's a tiny word, the word 'us'. The Lord says 'Who will go for us?' implying this is the call of the triune God, the Father, the Son and the Spirit who all beautifully coexist as one God calling Isaiah and us into this one story. For Isaiah, his AHA moment came to its zenith when he realised *his sin was worse than he thought, but the grace of God was greater than he hoped.*

Isaiah is now ready to become our time-travelling storyteller, the one who will guide us through the story of God from creator to redeemer to perfecter; the one who will lead us to rediscover our place in God's epic adventure story. Now we turn the page to part one of the story; first we head to the classroom. So let the story begin . . . after all, there is *no greater story.*

PART ONE

Creator

**Author, Inspirer, Originator,
Playwright . . .**

In the beginning there was nothing
No tradition
No religion
No sin
And no slaughter
Just a spirit
Resting above waters
Where no life was found
Could've checked with ultrasound
There's only ultra-silence
But rather than play a violin
The Spirit's painting in ultraviolet
Picturing the Amazon before Bezos
Speaking existence into the chaos
A king, emerging from the eremos
Darkness can't bear his cadence
So light bears witness
Of six days moving with persistence
His voice a quiet insistence
Against damnation
The resistance cries what in tarnation
But this is love's incarnation
If the temple was Solomon's innovation
Then creation
Is the Son of Man's inspiration
Yet not a drop of perspiration
Fell from heaven
See on the seventh
Feet on the table
God is sabbathing
The whole of his earth was, tabernacling
And nature's banqueting

With the King whose ways are patient
You'd need a space ship
To catch praises rising like a fragrance
His name
Falling from the lips of ancients
El Shaddai
Adonai
Yahweh
Abba, our Father
Covered in glory
Yet he'd rather
Appoint sons and daughters
As his co-authors
Coordinators
In an orchestration
Saturated with his infatuation
The greatest story
Spoken in a father's diction
We come seeking a prescription
But leave with an inscription
Upon our hearts
The finger of God writes
We shall never be apart

The
Classroom

'To whom will you compare me?
Or who is my equal?' says the Holy One.
Lift up your eyes and look to the heavens:
who created all these?
He who brings out the starry host one by one
and calls forth each of them by name.
Because of his great power and mighty strength,
not one of them is missing.

(Isaiah 40:25-26)

I believe that each of us comes from the
creator trailing wisps of glory.

(Maya Angelou)[15]

CHAPTER ONE

God at the Beginning

Every story has a beginning, a middle and an end, but every great story has much more than that. It has drama, intrigue, suspense, emotion, surprise, maybe a little comedy or romance, but above all connection.

The story must connect with us if it is to really matter to us.

Everybody has a story and everybody's story matters. Nobody gets the story they really want, but here's the amazing truth: everybody's story can find meaning and purpose when it's part of a bigger story . . . a greater story. Isaiah is our time-travelling storyteller unpacking the greater story of God, and like an Old Testament Doctor Who, he will dip in and out of time and sequence as he touches on the key headlines of God's greater story. In the process we will look for the connection, the part where the story relates to us, and the part we are each called to play.

As the story begins, Isaiah takes us to the very beginning and to one of the central themes running through the book of

Isaiah, namely creation and re-creation. This idea that God is the originator of the story is incredibly important. The very first words of the Bible recorded in Genesis read: 'In the beginning God created the heavens and the earth' (Genesis 1:1).

Then in the Genesis narrative God breathes his life into the first man, and man is created 'in his own image' (Genesis 1:27), and this is incredibly important to the story we are considering. The point of an image is to image, it's to reflect and point towards something or someone else. Creation is God's plan A and all of creation including humankind is to point to and reflect the Creator. Creation is God's great and grand idea as a gift to himself that all of creation might reflect the glory of God, and also as a gift to humankind that we would enjoy God and his creation, as it says in the famous words of the Westminster Catechism, 'Man's chief end is to glorify God and enjoy him for ever.'[16] This idea is then picked up in the first few words of the New Testament when John declares, 'In the beginning was the Word' (John 1:1).

The word used here is *'logos'*, which in biblical understanding is thought to mean the embodiment of an idea, the expression of a thought, and Jesus becomes the means through which the creational idea and motif is fully expressed and comes to fruition. All through the Bible this idea of creation and re-creation pulls us back to the central thought that this story was and is God's plan A, there is no plan B!

Isaiah constantly points his audience to the creation then the exodus from captivity where the people of God came through the Red Sea as almost a moment of re-creation. He also uses the exile they find themselves in as another hint towards re-creation. It's as if he is saying, 'I built the house, you pulled it down, but I will rebuild it again.' He opens up the book by referencing the heavens and the earth even though he is addressing the present rebellion and failure of the people of

God: 'Hear me, you heavens! Listen, earth! For the LORD has spoken: "I reared children and brought them up, but they have rebelled against me"' (Isaiah 1:2).

The 'heavens and the earth' are a recurring theme throughout Isaiah as are other images, pictures and metaphors that point to a God who as Creator not only authors and originates the story but is still at work within that story; he is kind of like the playwright dreaming, conceiving, birthing and producing the story. It's a story of hope and good news. The Creator is also the re-creator, the exodus and the exile point to future fulfilment, as if Isaiah is saying, 'God has done it before. He will do it again.'

All the time he references creation he is urging people (and us) to look to the Creator beyond the creation. Often attributed to Confucius is the powerful saying, 'The wise man points at the moon, only the fool looks at the finger.'[17]

What are some of the other recurring creation themes Isaiah references?

'Mountains' appear throughout the book (2:2-3; 11:9; 40:4-5; 41:15-16; 52:7) as do 'waters and seas' (11:9; 43:2). Both these images combine to demonstrate not only the power and majesty of the Creator but that the future will be glorious: 'They will neither harm nor destroy on all my holy mountain, for the earth will be filled with the knowledge of the LORD as the waters cover the sea' (Isaiah 11:9).

The frequent references to the grandeur of creation encourage and invite people to look up, to not allow their current circumstances to determine their faith, their hope or their outlook.

The 'up look' should inform the 'outlook'.

'Lions' are also a recurring theme in Isaiah's message (11:6; 35:9; 38:13) and I can't help but let my mind go to one of the greatest stories of the twentieth century, *The Lion, the Witch, and the Wardrobe.* In this enigmatic and enthralling story, C.S. Lewis' depiction of the lion Aslan is a type and representation of Jesus. As Beaver famously says of Aslan, 'Course he isn't safe. But he's good. He's the King, I tell you.'[18] The King will emerge as the story unfolds.

Another key idea Isaiah frequently references is the idea of God as our 'Maker' (17:7; 54:5). He then combines that idea with another idea immediately accessible to his audience, that of a potter and the clay:

> Woe to those who quarrel with their Maker, those who are nothing but potsherds among the potsherds on the ground. Does the clay say to the potter, 'What are you making?' Does your work say, 'The potter has no hands?'

(Isaiah 45:9)

This relationships between Creator and created, between potter and clay is a constant theme of Scripture, and so crucial that we never forget whose hand is on our life and that he has not just created the world then taken his hand off it, but he remains involved, shaping, forming, creating and recreating.

The other goal of this broad-sweep approach Isaiah is taking is to remind his audience that the greater story originates in the heart, mind and will of God the Creator. We often describe God in human terms as does Isaiah (technically it's called anthropomorphism) and that's OK, but let's remember God is not just a better version of us, an upgrade, if you like, he is a completely different being and entity.

He doesn't just love, he *is* love.

He doesn't just do good things, he *is* goodness.

He doesn't just demonstrate compassion, he *is* compassion.

Isaiah's goal here is to remind the people of the distinctions between the Creator and the created. The creature is not greater than the Creator, the clay is not greater than the potter, and far from this being a lesson in 'know your place', this is actually a call to trust, an invitation to lay aside fear and a challenge to rediscover our place in the epic adventure of God.

As helpful as a broad sweep might be, the classroom is where we take a deeper dive into Isaiah.

So, if you have your oxygen tanks ready ... let's dive ...

Isaiah 40 is where our storyteller makes the turn.

The context for this chapter is we are now in the reign of King Jehoiachin (586–560 BC) and the period of fighting and turbulence is coming to an end. Some of God's people are settling in exile, others are struggling to settle in that exile, but the pressing concern is that the city of Jerusalem is in ruins. As bleak as things look, Isaiah is a storyteller with some good news; in fact, some great news. Chapters 1–39 are mostly about judgement, chapters 40–66 are mostly about comfort, hope and good news. Chapter 40 begins almost like an overture to a symphony, melodies and harmonies combining in cascading references to this magnificent story of God; creation, redemption and ultimately, perfection. Within this music the central motif rings loud and clear: 'To whom [or to what] will you compare me?' Isaiah begins with the word 'comfort' (Isaiah 40:25) which he repeats: 'Comfort, comfort my people, says your God' (Isaiah 40:1).

The Hebrew word for 'comfort' here is *nacham* which means 'to console, to have pity and compassion'.[19] It carries the idea of a deep sigh, almost like God taking a deep breath, and isn't that comforting in itself, as I'm sure we all know what it is to take some deep breaths these days? Isaiah then references things that are to unfold in this great story, which we will get to, but then he spends time around a central idea expressed in verse 12:

> Who has measured the waters in the hollow of his hand, or with the breadth of his hand marked off the heavens? Who has held the dust of the earth in a basket, or weighed the mountains on the scales and the hills in a balance?
>
> (Isaiah 40:12)

God seems to love these rhetorical questions and, of course, Jesus was a master of them! Questions asked by God are powerful because they are never about him finding out the answers but always about us finding out who we are, where we are and how we move to where he wants us to be. Isaiah is articulating the truth that if God is Creator, he made all that is made, so he is more than able to care for us, to provide for us and to hold our lives together. Picture a God holding the dust of the earth in his hands; now picture all your troubles in those same hands . . . now that's comfort. He is not finished with the questions and so goes again in verse 21:

> Do you not know? Have you not heard? Has it not been told you from the beginning? Have you not understood since the earth was founded?
>
> (Isaiah 40:21)

Are you getting it yet? Is the message coming through? Your life finds its identity, its meaning and its purpose in relation to the one who created you, and that's God. Look up and see how vast he is, the stars, 'the circle of the earth' as Isaiah references in verse 22. This could also be called the outer rim, the edges of the known universe. It's as if God is saying, 'I am beyond all of what you see, know and grasp, yet am also within, closer than the air you breathe.' Isaiah then reminds his audience earthly power and human leaders are both temporary and transitory.

John Watts in his commentary on Isaiah says, 'Nothing in human existence is as fragile as power. God can take it away in an instant.'[20]

An example of this is found in human history, namely Caesar Augustus, the adopted son of Julius Caesar. As Julius Caesar was referred to as a god so his adopted son was known as a 'son of the god'. Interesting that all the world really knows of him now is as a footnote in the story of the birth of Jesus (Luke 2:1).

I'm reminded of the story of the French philosopher Voltaire who reportedly once said, 'One hundred years from my day, there will not be a Bible on the earth except one that is looked upon by an antiquarian curiosity-seeker.'[21] Some hundred years later, Voltaire's house was being used to print Bibles. Whether this is a story based on fact or fiction is contentious, but needless to say, many once powerful leaders, empires, dynasties, philosophies and ideologies have come and gone and the Creator continues, as does his story.

Isaiah then drives the message home even deeper as he then invites his audience to shift their gaze from earthly leaders to heavenly stars:

'To whom will you compare me? Or who is my equal?' says the Holy One. Lift up your eyes and look to the heavens: who created all these? He who brings out the starry host one by one and calls forth each of them by name. Because of his great power and mighty strength, not one of them is missing.

(Isaiah 40:25-26)

It's as if God through Isaiah is giving his audience and us a challenge, 'If I created all these stars, surely I can create a way in your life? If I can hold galaxies in place, surely I can hold your life together?' Isaiah is trying to open up the imagination of his audience because he knows God has something big to put into their minds and . . . *you can't fit big dreams in small minds.*

The word 'created' here is so important; it's a rare word in the original Hebrew language but it does occur in Genesis 1 and 2. The word is *bara* and means, 'formed, fashioned, shaped'. John Watts in his commentary on this chapter suggests the word 'create' in its original meaning is supported by other overlapping words which convey the ideas of *found, form, make and stabilise.* He puts all this into focus and meaning when he says, 'All of these portray God as actively creating, forming, shaping, and stabilising the universe and the historical social order from the beginning on into the present. There is no place for chaos or lack of control, in either sphere. God is in control. And this Creator, Maker, Stabiliser is identical with Israel's Saviour and Redeemer who has willed that Jerusalem be restored.'[22]

Isaiah is encouraging his audience to 'look up' to see their God again as Creator, Maker, Originator and Author before he then zooms in on their major complaint, that God doesn't see them: 'Why do you complain, Jacob? Why do you say, Israel, "My way

is hidden from the Lord; my cause is disregarded by my God"?'
(Isaiah 40:27).

Or let me put it in a way each and every one of us can relate to:
*God, are you there, God, do you care, God, can you do anything
about this?* How many of us have asked, are asking, or will
ask these same questions in our story? We will look at these
questions in the living room as we journey together.

As Isaiah draws this 'overture' to a close, he reminds us all of
two life-changing attributes of our greater God; that he is both
consistent and persistent.

*God is a God who plays the long game ...
God is a God who never runs out of steam ...*

Do you not know? Have you not heard? The Lord is the
everlasting God, the Creator of the ends of the earth.
He will not grow tired or weary, and his understanding
no one can fathom.

(Isaiah 40:28)

What does all this mean for us?

Before we get to that, and we will, I sense Isaiah would want
us to linger in the classroom for a few more minutes; it's not
that we need to stay back after class, it's just that there's a bit
more theory we need to grasp. If the story starts with God as
Creator, many Christians have begun to lose their confidence
in this truth. In the face of scepticism and science, we fear
that a view of creation that originates from a Creator is now
outdated and has been replaced by reason and rationale.

This couldn't be further from the truth.

Science and faith are not mutually exclusive, polar opposites, or diametrically opposed. In many ways they are two sides of the same coin; one may tell us *how* but the other tells us *why*.

I get twitchy when I sense Christians are either fearful or defensive when it comes to faith and science; we shouldn't be either. In fact, the vast majority of Nobel Prize winners are either Christians or from the Jewish tradition, with relatively few self-declared atheists or agnostics.

Dr Robert Jastrow, professor of astronomy and director of the Mount Wilson Institute, puts it this way:

> Now we see how the astronomical evidence leads to a biblical view of the origin of the world . . . for the scientist who has lived by his faith in the power of reason, the story ends like a bad dream. He has scaled the mountains of ignorance, he is about to conquer the highest peak; as he pulls himself over the final rock, he is greeted by a band of theologians who have been sitting there for centuries.[23]

I for one would like to think Isaiah would be sat there right alongside them!

For too long we've felt intimidated by the vociferous voices baying for rationale and reason that they assert will once and for all destroy the notion of faith. We've at times felt like those proverbial grasshoppers cowering before the giants of academia, but Isaiah takes us into the classroom to teach us a lesson: Look up . . . your God is greater!

But what about the how?

There are so many brilliant minds over the centuries who have grappled with these issues, and much has been written by them and others trying to bring together science and faith in the *how* of creation. Let me point us to three main areas for consideration.

Something or nothing?

The most recent discoveries of science are turning us back towards the idea that the universe had a point of origin. The Hubble telescope enables us to see further away than ever before. The light from those faraway galaxies takes such a long time to reach us, it's like a time machine; we're seeing what the universe looked like just after its birth in the 'Big Bang'. The Big Bang was first proposed by Georges Lemaître (a Belgian priest and astronomer!) in 1920.[24] It isn't a problem for Christians, it's just saying that the universe began from a single point and has been expanding ever since.

There was nothing, then there was something; science and faith can both line up behind this.

The issue is, how did the universe come into being and subsequently creation as we know and experience – the mountains, the waters, the seas, the trees, the animals and ultimately the people that Isaiah speaks about. Some would assert this idea . . . Did it happen? Yes . . . What caused it? Nothing . . . *So nothing caused something out of nothing?*

Francis Collins, former director of the National Human Genome Research Institute writes:

> The Big Bang cries out for a divine explanation . . . it forces the conclusion that nature had a defined beginning. I cannot see how nature could have created itself. Only a supernatural force that is outside of space and time could have done that.[25]

Design or disorder?

Let me put this in simple terms that I can grasp ... how do we explain such an intricate, mysterious, beautiful, awe-inspiring creation if we only have mere chance as a possible explanation?

Imagine someone throwing a dart from the far side of the universe and it not only hits a dartboard the other side of the universe, but it hits the bullseye? That would take some faith to believe that!

The old illustration I used to deploy in schools back in the day (before smartphones and actually before anything smart!) centred around a cow taking a stroll one day:

> Imagine a cow walking down the street and there's a glass factory, a steel factory and a jewellers' in the street. All of a sudden there's a huge explosion, the cow flies into the air (no animals were harmed in the making of this illustration) along with the three factories, and after the dust had settled there on the ground was a perfectly formed and functioning watch. The leather strap from the cow, the glass the steel and the jewels from their various factories all randomly coming together to form a perfectly working watch.

How much faith would you need to believe that?

Then there's one final area of thinking for us to consider ...

Monkey-kind or humankind?

The third area to consider when thinking of creation is the humanness of humans. Where does human personality come from? Where do existential questions about identity, meaning and purpose come from? Can you imagine the animals at the watering hole in the Serengeti one day and the buffalo says to the antelope, 'What have I done with my life?' The hyenas say, 'Since the cubs have left home, I don't know who I am anymore.' Or the hippo nervously says to the lion, 'Does my bum look big in this?'

There's something uniquely ... well ... *human* about humans; how did that happen?

It is amazing how much DNA humans share with chimpanzees, but does that mean we would be OK sharing a long train journey sat next to one, or trust them to babysit our kids? I suggest not!

Maybe my favourite thought along this line comes from C.S. Lewis who was an atheist but became a believer in the greater story of God. He puts it this way: 'My argument against God was that the universe seemed so cruel and unjust. But how had I got this idea of just and unjust? A man does not call a line crooked unless he has some idea of a straight line.'[26]

Maybe a more compelling reason to embrace the Creator and his story is not the *how* but the *why* ... Why did God create?

Love

Let that sink in, but as you do, bear in mind Isaiah would invite us to go further . . . in his exhortation to the people of God, he's inviting them to look up and see that the one who holds the stars in his hands holds their lives in those same hands. This God can be known, loved and trusted. This is the comfort we all seek deep down which gives us our identity, meaning and purpose, and with that comes real and robust hope. The hope that our story can be redeemed and we find who we are and what we were created for within the greater story of God.

Now we need to see what difference the Creator makes to this greater story we are invited to play our part in. We need to move from the *what* to the *so what* . . . we need to move from the *classroom* to the *living room* and as we do, let's try to find some inspiration as we consider how we live out this greater story.

The
Living Room

CHAPTER TWO

Greater Than Our Understanding

'I don't think the way you think. The way you work isn't the way I work.' GOD's Decree. 'For as the sky soars high above earth, so the way I work surpasses the way you work, and the way I think is beyond the way you think.'

(Isaiah 55:8-9, *The Message*)

For I do not seek to understand in order that I may believe, but I believe in order to understand.

(St Anselm)[27]

'I just don't get it, it doesn't make any sense to me!' Have you ever found yourself saying something like this, or something very similar? What happened or is happening just doesn't add up for you, and then you find yourself saying to God, 'If you really are the great Creator God, are you still in control?' What happens to our faith when we don't understand, and what happens to the story when our minds cannot grasp what is happening around us?

The people who heard Isaiah's prophecy must have had similar thoughts as the prophet began to speak about a future ruler who the Lord was going to use to bring about his purposes, His name was Cyrus, a Persian king who would go on to conquer Babylon and help the first group of Jews return from exile:

> This is what the LORD says to his anointed, to Cyrus, whose right hand I take hold of to subdue nations before him and to strip kings of their armour, to open doors before him so that gates will not be shut.
>
> (Isaiah 45:1)

Isaiah goes on in this chapter to reference creation, and even uses the potter and the clay analogy as he did in other parts of the book, but now he is referencing the Persian king Cyrus. So he (the potter) will use an 'ungodly' king (the clay) in his purposes for his people? In the words of a once famous tennis player, 'You cannot be serious!'[28]

But when you are the author of the story, you get to hold the pen . . .

In this greater story of God, where we are called to play our part, there will be many moments when we don't understand what God appears to be doing, or not doing. In this greater story of God, the world around us and within us at times will be confusing, bewildering, disorientating, and it's in those moments that we are tempted to become small and play it safe. We lose that sense of God being in control and God being in charge; God is greater than our understanding.

In 2015, the church I lead had already been in a building programme for many years. We had experienced great days and disappointing days, victories and setbacks. Our desire to expand our building was so we could reach more people with the good news of the gospel, and we were on the threshold of a new opportunity at last.

Then came the fire . . .

I had just been on an overseas trip and got back late Saturday evening, so was sound asleep at 5 a.m. Sunday, when my wife woke me, saying, 'The church is on fire, the church is on fire!' Now, I'm a Pentecostal, so murmured through my sleep, 'Amen, it's about time!' Then I realised she was talking about a literal fire. As I ran across the road towards the church, I will never forget that moment when I saw a quarter of the West Midlands fire service at our building and flames lighting up the early morning sky. In the weeks and months afterwards, there were many moments I said to God, 'You cannot be serious!' There were many times I was confused, bewildered and disorientated. I didn't understand and I couldn't comprehend. Now, some time later and with the gift of hindsight, it's a different story; in the years since the fire, we've changed our name, got a new building, launched several other expressions of church and grown in so many ways. Did God cause the fire? No, that was an electrical fault. Has God shown that he is still the Creator whose ways are higher than our ways? Absolutely.

So, as we play our part in this greater story, how do we live it out when we don't understand?

Do what you know to be true

When we can't see the whole picture, let's make sure we do the parts we know are in the picture. Those things we know are true, let's keep doing those. As a pastor in the same church for more than thirty years, I've been through many ups and downs of life and people's lives. I've married couples who've survived against seemingly great odds, and I've buried way too many people who were taken far too young. In those painful and confusing moments, I've often tried to hold on to the verses right at the end of Deuteronomy 29:

> The secret things belong to the LORD our God, but the things revealed belong to us and to our children for ever, that we may follow all the words of this law.
>
> (Deuteronomy 29:29)

Rather than get bent out of shape with what we don't understand or can't comprehend, why not put those things in a box called 'secret things that belong to God'? Instead, let's focus on the things we do know, the things revealed to us that will not only bring peace of mind, but also evidence our trust in our Maker, the Creator, the one who holds the pen to his story and to ours. The problem many of us experience is, we can't see the full picture. Many years ago, a friend of mine's wife went into hospital to give birth to their second child. A mistake was made in the hospital and she died on the operating table, even though their daughter lived. I remember when I heard the news, immediately getting on a plane to be with him, not knowing what to say or do. I will never forget the words he said to me that day we met; he said, 'It's like my face is pressed up close to an oil painting; all I can see are images and colours, no real picture, but in time, as I move further back, maybe a picture will emerge.' Of course, the reality is, sometimes we never see the full picture this side of eternity, but that is because God is greater than our understanding and some things remain mysteries to us. We can still do what we know to be true and there's something else we can do . . .

Look for the hand, not just the plan

The three words Jesus often loved to say were, 'Come, follow me' (for example, Matthew 4:19). He said those words to fisherman and tax collectors, he said them to rich men and poor women, and he says those same three words to us. They are words a rabbi would say; they are an invitation to a life of imitation, they are words of access to an adventure. Here's the challenge . . . if Jesus said to me, 'Come, follow me', my first response would most likely be, 'Where are we going?' or, 'What will I need?' or, 'Will there be Wi-Fi?'

These types of responses reveal our propensity to want to know the plan before we trust the person. When it comes to faith, when it comes to the adventure of God's greater story, it doesn't work that way. Dr Martin Luther King Jr famously said, 'Faith is taking the next step even when you don't see the whole staircase.'[29]

As you take that step of faith remember this powerful truth: *God's timing is an expression of God's kindness.*

I was taught a powerful lesson recently in a season of frustration and confusion. In the past few years, we have seen many people become Christians at our church, with many of those from an unchurched or de-churched background. We have had powerful baptism celebrations and been inspired by some great stories. Yet we have also seen several of these people, many younger women, diagnosed with serious health issues, and several of them have died in recent months. I remember walking out of one hospice after my wife and I sat holding the hands of a lady who only got baptised less than a year previously. As we read the Bible over her and prayed with her, we knew it would be the last time we saw her this side of eternity. I left that hospice a little angry and confused: 'God, why didn't you heal her? She had just come into a relationship with you and with our church family. It doesn't make sense?' Then a few days later, I heard an amazing talk where the preacher said something along these lines: in times of confusion and uncertainty, don't lose sight of the fact that God's timing is an expression of God's kindness. The cancer was coming back anyway, that painful situation, that crisis was coming anyway, but in the kindness of God, this lady knew Jesus and now had a community of faith who went in to see her every one of her final days on earth. Imagine how those final days would have been for her without Jesus, without the church and without the hope?

What happens when we do all we know to be true, when we do seek God's hand, not just his plan, when we do remember his timing is his kindness but still find ourselves in a place where life is beyond our understanding?

For many years, I, and we as a church, have been involved with Balkan countries, notably Bulgaria and Albania. On one of my first trips to Durres, Albania, I met a young couple I'd heard a lot about. Tani and his wife, Elona, and their two small children were leading a church in the north of Albania. Through a tragic set of circumstances, Tani had become part of the blood feud, an ancient practice still in operation in that part of the world based on vengeance for wrongs done to families. Through no fault of their own, they were now in the blood feud, and every day was a day to look over their shoulders if they ever left the house, which was very rare. During one of my early visits, they had sneaked out of their house in the middle of the night to travel more than two hours to be at our conference. As I listened to their story, as I got to know them, their faith and confidence in God, I couldn't help but be impacted. They were pastoring a church and raising a family in the toughest of circumstances. They eventually left for safety in England, but while there, Tani felt God speak to him about returning home and continuing the story God had called them into. So, they did, and then on 8 October 2010, after locking up the church one Friday lunchtime, Tani was shot and killed in the streets by a young man from the other family. I have watched over the years as Elona embraced the responsibility of leading the church, something very uncommon for a woman in that culture. I have watched her and her amazing children learn to forgive the family who killed Tani, how they have set up a charitable organisation to support families in the blood feud, and lobbied governments all around the world about this injustice still going on in this part of their country. I have sat in houses where men have been recently killed and watched as they wept and asked Elona to explain how she could forgive the people who took her husband. I have sat in awe hearing her talk about what Jesus had done for them, and the forgiveness they have received, which enables them to extend that forgiveness to other people. It hasn't always been easy; there was a day when Elona's young son asked his mum about the man who killed his daddy. Gabriel then said to his mum, 'We will forgive him, that's what God would want us to do.' Elona has subsequently prayed with presidents, debated with philosophers, lobbied politicians, served and cared for families in the most tragic circumstances, along with her incredible church I've had the privilege of standing alongside for many years. Will they ever fully understand what happened, and why Tani's life was cut short on that day all those many years ago? I doubt they will, but their lives are living testimony to the God who is greater than our understanding, the God who redeems our story, even the one we don't want, and brings something beautiful and powerful out of it. He is the Creator.

As you step into God's epic adventure story, there will be many days where you lack understanding, where you don't know what's happening or what may happen next, where what's around the corner is unknown and unpredictable. On days like that, look up at the stars or the mountains and ask yourself, 'Who made these?' It's the same God who made you, our Creator, Maker and Author, and he has it covered.

- God is greater than our understanding, where do you lack understanding right now?

- What's the next step you need to take as you pursue God's greater story?

A prayer for when we struggle to understand

Lord, there are times I'm at a loss for words.
I struggle to understand and comprehend,
Things seem beyond me ...
But in those moments, help me realise that's OK because nothing is beyond you.
You are greater than my understanding, your thoughts are higher than my thoughts.
Help me to trust you in the not knowing and put my hope in you in the waiting.
Help me to look for your timing and acknowledge it as an expression of your kindness.
Help me to draw close to you, the Creator, Sustainer and the Author who holds the pen.
For you are greater than my understanding.

Amen

CHAPTER THREE

Greater Than Our Fears

So do not fear, for I am with you; do not be dismayed,
for I am your God. I will strengthen you and help you;
I will uphold you with my righteous right hand.

(Isaiah 41:10)

The presence of fear does not mean you have no faith.
Fear visits everyone but make your fear a visitor and not
a resident.

(Max Lucado)[30]

The most searched for Bible verse on the Bible app in 2023
and for the third time in four years was Isaiah 41:10, and the
most searched for word was 'hope'. There's something about
fear that affects our sense of hope. When what's in front of
us appears greater than what seems inside of us, we can soon
lose hope. The people Isaiah was communicating to knew all
about this, as they had suffered conquest and exile; they knew
about displacement and loss of status and security. Like all
of us, they had experienced how disappointment can lead to
discouragement and they needed hope.

Throughout the Bible the most frequent exhortation is 'do not fear', but we still do.

Jesus exhorts us to 'not worry' (Matthew 6:25) – it adds nothing to our life, but we still do. Here's where we miss something really important: worry and fear are part of the human condition. It does nothing to our wellbeing or our faith when we simply feel guilty about experiencing worry and fear. Fear and faith are not mutually exclusive, polar opposite, or diametrically opposed. Fear and faith can coexist if we understand *God is greater than our fears*.

In his helpful book, *If You Want to Walk on Water, You Have to Get Out of the Boat*[31] author John Ortberg talks about fear being part of the human condition. He talks about how fear affects us physically, mentally and emotionally, and how research suggests some of us may have a predisposition towards greater fear and anxiety because we have a certain gene. I can guarantee some of you reading this now think you have that gene!

Isaiah picks up the fear theme again in Isaiah 43 when he says:

> But now, this is what the LORD says –
> he who created you, Jacob,
> he who formed you, Israel:
> 'Do not fear, for I have redeemed you;
> I have summoned you by name; you are mine.
> When you pass through the waters,
> I will be with you;
> and when you pass through the rivers,
> they will not sweep over you.
> When you walk through the fire,
> you will not be burned;
> the flames will not set you ablaze.
> For I am the LORD your God,

the Holy One of Israel, your Saviour;
I give Egypt for your ransom,
Cush and Seba in your stead.
Since you are precious and honoured in my sight,
and because I love you,
I will give people in exchange for you,
nations in exchange for your life.
Do not be afraid, for I am with you;
I will bring your children from the east
and gather you from the west.

(Isaiah 43:1-5)

Notice Isaiah doesn't say *'if'* you pass through the waters or the fire, he says *'when'*. It's not a possibility, it's a certainty. With that certainty there will be fear, but what's a greater certainty than that is this . . .

God is greater than our fears

In Matthew 14, we find one of the most famous and powerful stories that demonstrates how God is greater than our fears. The disciples found themselves at sea, again! They were used to the sea; after all, many were fisherman. But this particular night on the Sea of Galilee, they found themselves out of their depth. The storm was instant, unexpected, unusual, unprecedented even. In the middle of those stormy waters, Jesus invited them to leave their boat and to come to him. Jesus invited them to the adventure of walking with him upon the very waters that threatened to drown them. This is a part of the greater story of God we are invited into, the epic adventure of trusting him. Matthew records it this way:

But Jesus immediately said to them: 'Take courage! It is I. Don't be afraid.'

'Lord, if it's you,' Peter replied, 'tell me to come to you on the water.'

'Come,' he said.

(Matthew 14:27-29)

Peter was the only one who responded to the invitation to trust Jesus. He was also the only one who subsequently took his eyes off Jesus and started to sink. He was also the only one rescued by Jesus and therefore the only one who had stories to tell when he got back into the boat, wet but exhilarated! We each have a choice to choose what stories we want to tell in the future, ones where we stayed dry but have nothing to say, or where we got a little wet but our faith grew and we encountered Jesus along the way.

One of the joys of my life is when I get to see the Church around the world, and one of my all-time favourite places is Albania. We have a church we help lead in Durres, Albania, and the word for fear is *frike*, which when I hear it pronounced in Albanian sounds like 'freak'.

Here's my thought concerning fear . . . *It's OK to freak out sometimes because God is greater than our fears.*

There was so much freaking out on the lake that particular evening. Our Sunday school view of this story has us picture a tranquil lake with a gentle storm brewing, but in reality, the disciples were in a horrendous storm for hours and fearing for their lives. They were freaking out.

Then they saw what appeared to be a ghost but was actually Jesus. They were freaking out.

Then Peter walked on the water and began to sink. He was freaking out.

Here's the good news, here's the hope ... *It's OK to freak out sometimes because God is greater than our fears.*

So, as we get to play our part in this greater story, how do we react in the living room of life when we find ourselves freaking out?

When you're freaking out, don't try harder, trust deeper

Our natural inclination in times of fear is to try to take control of the situation, or of others. We try harder, and yet any lifeguard will tell you the response they would prefer if you were in trouble in the water and they were trying to rescue you is not that you try harder, but that you trust deeper. It's in those moments of fear and anxiety when we get to choose to trust God and open our hands rather than to clench our fists and try to go it alone.

When you're freaking out, remember growth is always on the other side

It's easy to be critical of Peter, who took his eyes off Jesus, but remember he is the only one who had the faith to get out of the boat. He is also the only one who had some stories to tell when he got back into the boat. As Florence Nightingale said, 'How very little can be done under the spirit of fear.'[32]

Fear can paralyse us, restrict us, contain us, but so can comfort and the love of playing it safe. When you find yourself freaking out, remind yourself growth is on the other side of the fear; nobody really grows in their comfort zone.

There's no growth in the comfort zone and no comfort in the growth zone.

When you're freaking out, make the turn

Another favourite country of mine is Bulgaria, and many years ago a friend of mine and I were speaking at a youth event on the Black Sea coast. Early one morning (and I mean really early), one of the young Bulgarian guys invited us to drive up the coast and swim with him in his favourite part of the Black Sea. Not wishing to be shamed in any way by this younger (and fitter) guy, we said, 'Sure let's do it!' Needless to say, what ensued was shameful for us as he dived into the sea and swam like a dolphin while my friend and I splashed around pathetically, resembling a cross between flailing toddlers and beached whales. As the currents got stronger, I was desperate for some sight of land and there it was, a huge rock emerging from the water calling my name!

That was my moment to choose – to stop letting the fear take me down or just try harder, or choose to turn and reach for the rock that would take me up. As David puts it in the Psalms, 'From the end of the earth I will cry to You, When my heart is overwhelmed; Lead me to the rock that is higher than I' (Psalm 61:2, NKJV).

When we get freaked out, we can choose to make that crucial turn to go higher rather than allow the fear to take us lower. When we are overwhelmed, we can reach for a God who is never overwhelmed.

The only thing insurmountable is God

You may be saying, 'I'm freaked out right now, I'm at the end of my rope, I feel like I'm sinking, even drowning ... what do I do?' Let go of the belief that you have to hold it all together, because God is greater than your fears, and make the turn, reach for the rock that is higher, that is greater.

An anecdotal story that may or may not be true makes a really good point. It allegedly took place a century or so ago when a ship in a storm crashed against the cliffs of Cornwall at the south-west corner of England. A fifteen-year-old sailor swam to safety on an offshore rock. He climbed up and waited all night until he was rescued the next morning. A reporter interviewed him and commented, 'You must have been shaking all night as you clung to that rock? 'Yes,' the sailor replied. 'I trembled all night with fear and cold.' Then he added, 'But the rock never trembled once.'

It's OK to freak out sometimes because God is greater than our fears.

It's OK to freak out sometimes because God is the rock who never trembles.

- In what areas of your life are you freaking out right now?

- In what ways can you make the turn and reach for the rock that is higher?

A prayer for when fear threatens to take us down

Lord, when fear threatens to take me under, help me to lean on you.
When worry and anxiety threaten to choke the breath out of my lungs, I raise a cry of praise.
When all I see and sense is scary, I choose to reach for the rock that is higher than I.
For you are greater than my fears.

Amen

CHAPTER FOUR

Greater Than Our Limitations

Do you not know?
Have you not heard?
The LORD is the everlasting God,
the Creator of the ends of the earth.
He will not grow tired or weary,
and his understanding no one can fathom.
He gives strength to the weary
and increases the power of the weak.
Even youths grow tired and weary,
and young men stumble and fall;
but those who hope in the LORD
will renew their strength.
They will soar on wings like eagles;
they will run and not grow weary,
they will walk and not be faint.

(Isaiah 40:28-31)

And I too may construct my better world, for I am a child of God and an inheritor of a fragment of the mind that created all worlds.

(Helen Keller, author and disability activist who was both visually and hearing impaired)[33]

As Part One of this epic story of God draws to a close, we reflect again on what it means to rediscover our place in this adventure. To help us with this, let's return to the overture that is Isaiah 40 and linger on the final few verses. Here we read of a Creator God who gives us what we do not possess. With all of our resources, our technologies and even our AI, we are unable to access that which we desire and require the most, the breath of God. The promise here is of a Creator who longs to share his breath with his creation and in doing so, share the strength that enables us to overcome our natural limitations and play our part in the greater story of God.

These beautiful and poetic words contain timeless and eternal truths that if we can learn how to apply them to our lives, can result in a life that thrives rather than just survives. In verse 31, the word 'hope' seems to leap out of the page and yet many of us are listening for the word 'wait', as that is how many translations render this word.

So which is it, hope or wait? The answer is YES . . . Both!

The original word in Hebrew is *qavah* pronounced 'kaw-vaw' and it means 'wait for, enduring for, looking patiently for' with the idea of almost twisting and stretching in the waiting, or you might even say in the hoping. The two concepts of wait and hope almost overlap in this word and so it becomes *waiting hope and hopeful waiting.*

The New Living Translation throws in the word 'trust' and that fits with the idea of waiting hope or hopeful waiting because at its essence it all has to do with trust. This is in direct contrast to Israel's (and can I suggest our) insistence on God acting decisively and quickly. 'God teach me patience, and teach it to me now!'

When you know the Creator and when his breath is in you by his Spirit, he allows you to wait hopefully, to trust enduringly, and as we learn to do this, we receive the breath and the strength of God. This enables us to rise above the moment, even the cultural moment we find ourselves in, and to live from a different vantage point. His breath enables us to keep walking when we feel we can't take another step, to keep loving when we can't muster another kind word, and to even keep running when all we want to do is collapse!

This passage is in direct response to the 'complaint' of the people in verse 27, 'Why do you complain, Jacob? Why do you say, Israel, "My way is hidden from the LORD; my cause is disregarded by my God"?' (Isaiah 40:27).

Let's see it from *The Message* version and then we might say 'AHA, now I see myself there . . .'

Why would you ever complain, O Jacob,
or, whine, Israel, saying,
'GOD has lost track of me.
He doesn't care what happens to me'?
Don't you know anything? Haven't you been listening?
GOD doesn't come and go. God *lasts*.
He's Creator of all you can see or imagine.
He doesn't get tired out, doesn't pause to catch his breath.
And he knows *everything*, inside and out.
He energizes those who get tired,
gives fresh strength to dropouts.
For even young people tire and drop out,
young folk in their prime stumble and fall.
But those who wait upon GOD get fresh strength.
They spread their wings and soar like eagles,
They run and don't get tired,
they walk and don't lag behind.

(Isaiah 40:27-31)

You have never complained to God or even whined, have you? You have never raged against your circumstances or limitations and said 'if only God', have you? If you haven't, I know I have ... often. We can want to enter the story, to play our full part in the story, but then our limitations and frustrations smack us in the face and we lose our energy, our vitality, ultimately our spiritual breath.

But take heart ... *God is greater than our limitations.*

How do we access the breath and life of God, even with our limitations?

We learn to wait better.

Honesty time – I'm terrible at waiting, patience is not a virtue that comes naturally to me and yet I know it's so important. It's a fruit of the Spirit (Galatians 5:22-23) and, what's more, research proves patience is good for you. It enables you to navigate changes, improve resilience, endure uncertainty, develop inner strength, reduce stress, achieve long-term goals, increase self-control and facilitate understanding.

Patience makes your life better and makes you better at life.

The problem is, it's hard to develop patience and it's usually a painful process.

I've already mentioned our youngest son, Simeon. When he was around two, we knew something was not quite as it should be; his eye contact was concerning, his speech wasn't really there. Eventually we were told the devastating news that he had a range of life-altering conditions that would mean he would never lead an independent life, and our lives as young parents and church leaders would be forever changed. Over the years we've had to learn to navigate trauma and the loss of the life we envisaged, and at times it's felt limiting and frustrating. We liken it to a soundtrack of grief that is always playing underneath our lives. Sometimes the soundtrack is quiet so we hardly notice, other times we can hardly hear anything but the soundtrack. There have been times we've said to God, 'Why' and 'what if . . .?' I'm sure many of you reading can identify . . . *Surely if we didn't have these limitations, we could play a bigger part in your story, God?*

Then in the learning to wait better, we've discovered the very breath of God . . . we've discovered that the God of creation plays the long game and his treasure is a different gold from ours. In the hopeful waiting, we've discovered the truth of Isaiah 45:3:

> And I will give you treasures hidden in the darkness – secret riches. I will do this so you may know that I am the Lord, the God of Israel, the one who calls you by name.
>
> (NLT)

We have discovered treasures in Simeon with all of his complications and limitations. We've discovered riches in other families as we have been able to empathise with their similar challenges. I think it's shaped us as a church community, where we now have lots of families with children with additional needs as well as many adopted and fostered children. Simeon has taught us about pain, hope, joy, sorrow and led us to places of richness and discovery far beyond anything we envisaged when we held him as a baby in our arms all those years ago.

Like many people, we have also prayed that these and other limitations would be taken away. If you resonate with that but are almost too afraid to admit it, you're in good company; in fact, some of the Bible heroes of both Old and New Testament would testify to this. Take two of the most well-known, Moses and the apostle Paul. In 2 Corinthians 11, Paul talks about some of his fragility, some of the setbacks and limitations he has experienced. Then in chapter 12, he opens up this idea of weakness and strength by being vulnerable about the one limitation that was never taken away (as far as we know):

> Therefore, in order to keep me from becoming conceited, I was given a thorn in my flesh, a messenger of Satan, to torment me. Three times I pleaded with the Lord to take it away from me. But he said to me, 'My grace is sufficient for you, for my power is made perfect in weakness.' Therefore I will boast all the more gladly about my weaknesses, so that Christ's power may rest on me.
>
> (2 Corinthians 12:7-9)

We aren't entirely sure what the 'thorn in the flesh' was that Paul is speaking about, and there have been so many theories that cover all things physical, emotional, spiritual and relational, but whatever it was, it was something that caused Paul pain, but it was also something that caused Paul to constantly go back to God as his Creator, Sustainer and Enabler. Whatever it was it meant Paul couldn't just rely on his intellect or natural brilliance but instead, trust in God. Sometimes what we see as a limitation is a blessing in disguise as it causes us to trust God and to be reliant on his power that comes to us by his Spirit. In fact, our 'weaknesses' and our 'limitations' almost become portals for God's power.

God is greater than our limitations

But we need to learn to wait better.

Waiting is not a passive process. We wait expectantly, we wait with a posture towards God and others, and as we wait, who we become while we wait is as important as what we are waiting for.

Then there's something else we can do ...

We can learn to soar higher

Isaiah gives us a powerful picture of life connected to the Creator by referencing soaring on wings like eagles. Why an eagle? An eagle is born with large, heavy wings, but rather than using their own strength, they fly by harnessing the power of the airborne currents. The eagle learns to wait and not always to leap, sometimes waiting for days to catch the right wind current. At times they will even seek out a storm rather than avoid it, because they know the flight the other side of those winds will be rich. Likewise, in our lives we can experience a God who is greater when we learn to wait on him, when we learn to rest in him and when we learn to move with his Spirit. The Hebrew word for 'spirit' most used in the Bible is the word *ruach*, which is also used in many places for the concept of breath. The breath or the *ruach* of God hovered over the waters in Genesis 1, and breathed life into the nostrils of Adam in Genesis 2. We also see this word in the valley of dry bones that the prophet Ezekiel sees in Ezekiel 37. The thread running through all these references is that God breathes life, and it's his life in us which is his Holy Spirit. We are created in the image of God, empowered by the breath of God, and sustained by the life and energy of God. The problem for us in living this story out is not the breath of God, it's often our inability to put up the sails!

Let me explain ...

In ancient maritime understanding there is a place on earth called the ITCZ (intertropical convergence zone) where trade winds come together creating a band of low pressure where there is no wind. It's where the phrase 'stuck in the doldrums' originates. Any ship caught there is in trouble as no amount of effort can make the wind blow. As Christians, we often find ourselves 'stuck in the doldrums' where our spiritual life feels flat, listless, lacking in energy. The Spirit of God is the breath of God, he is the wind in our sails; let's make sure our sails are up and we don't allow ourselves to drift into the doldrums. The best way to do this is to do what New Testament writers encourage us to do, to 'keep in step with the Spirit' (Galatians 5:25; see also Galatians 5:17). How do we do this?

We learn to partner more

Here is one more image from the book of Isaiah to help us when we face limitations, and it's found towards the end of the book:

> Then his people recalled the days of old,
> the days of Moses and his people –
> where is he who brought them through the sea,
> with the shepherd of his flock?
> Where is he who set
> his Holy Spirit among them,
> who sent his glorious arm of power
> to be at Moses' right hand,
> who divided the waters before them,
> to gain for himself everlasting renown . . .
>
> (Isaiah 63:11-12)

Isaiah again references the exodus (when Israel supernaturally travelled through the Red Sea out of captivity and towards their promised land).

This speaks of the re-creation God the Creator is always seeking and we will get to that, but don't miss this powerful picture of

Moses here. If you remember your Bible stories, Moses finds himself at an impasse, a severe limitation. Upwards of 2 million people looking to him, deserts either side, an Egyptian army in hot pursuit and the uncrossable Red Sea in front of him. What does God tell him to do? To stretch out his staff! I want you to imagine the scene; there's no keyboard player accompanying with the holy chords of G to C, there's no subtle lighting or atmospheric haze, there's just Moses feeling very human but also being very obedient. He stretches out his arm. Maybe the teenagers in the crowd are saying, 'Is he going fishing?' The whole scene doesn't look very anointed or powerful, it's almost ordinary, even comical. Then Isaiah uses a phrase, 'sent his glorious arm of power to be at Moses' right hand'.

God stretched out his arm alongside the arm of Moses.

At that point a miracle happened and the Red Sea parted; the limitations were overcome.

Here's the big question: 'Whose arm accomplished the miracle, was it God or Moses?'

Of course we know it was God, but in another sense, wasn't it both?

St Augustine put it this way: 'Without God, we cannot, without us, God will not.'[34]

God does what we cannot do and we do what God will not do

This is the beauty and mystery of learning to partner with a God who is both Creator and ... *greater*. When we reach out our hand, whether it's to love or to serve, to encourage or to forgive, to teach or to support, God stretches his arm of power alongside ours. God is GREATER than our limitations, he is the Lord of heaven and earth, he is the Maker, the Originator, the Creator.

I saw this powerfully in action when I met Dr Richmond Wandera. I was on a leaders' trip to Uganda with Compassion International,[35] an organisation we partner with as a local church, helping to lift children out of poverty all across the world. The specific trip was as part of the partnership between Spring Harvest and Compassion and it was the last day; in fact, we were on our way to the airport to return home when we met Richmond. We turned up at the site; it was vast with well-kept gardens, impressive facilities. Richmond welcomed us and then began to tell us his story. We were captivated. His story wasn't the story anyone would have wanted: born into poverty and tragedy when as an eight-year-old his father was shot and killed, growing up with his siblings having to do whatever he could to survive. The family found themselves living in a one-bedroom house and without the father's income they could no longer attend school. So many limitations in the natural, but then the story began to change as he described how they found their way to a Compassion project. There the local pastor invested in him and introduced him to Jesus, and all that was because a teenage girl from England had sponsored him as a child. Literally, God used those two people to change his life and the trajectory of his future. At the age of fourteen, Richmond accepted Jesus into his life; by sixteen all five of his siblings and his mother had also become Jesus followers.

Now years later, Richmond trains thousands of leaders across Africa, plants churches, creates health and wellbeing centres for pastors and is seeing God the Creator transform all the limitations of his origin story into something truly wonderful and life-giving. He pastors one of the fastest growing churches in the country and they plant around three churches every year. The phrase that impacted me the most, that I will never forget, is when he said something like this: 'When most people are lifted out of poverty, they run as far as they can from it, but when Jesus lifted me out of poverty, I ran back towards it to help lift others out of it, just as I had been lifted.' That individual sponsor stretched out her arm when Richmond was a child and God stretched his arm alongside. That local pastor stretched out his arm as he invested in Richmond as a child and God stretched his arm alongside. Now Richmond does the same on a daily basis and is seeing God write a new story, a greater story. When we reach out our arm, God partners with us; when our limitations are twinned with God's creative power, almost anything can happen by the power of his Spirit.

- What 'Red Sea' or limitations are you currently facing?
- In what way is God asking you to stretch out your arm right now?

A prayer for when limitations threaten to stop the story God is wanting to write in our lives

Lord, I am often all too aware of my limitations.
Help me understand that none of these are a surprise to you and you still choose me.
Help me to embrace you more as I learn to embrace the limitations.
Help me to learn to walk, run and to soar with your Spirit as I partner more with you for your glory.
For you are greater than my limitations.

Amen

The
Playground

For all the resources and links mentioned,
scan the code to visit
www.springharvest.org/resources/no-greater-story

CHAPTER FIVE

The Creator in the Playground

We've been in the classroom looking at the *what*, we've been in the living room looking at the *so what*, now we turn to the *now what* and we head to the playground where everyone gets to play their part in the greater story.

My life

We live in a world of comparison and competition. It causes us to envy what others have and often resent what we seem to be left with. We too often succumb to FOMO (fear of missing out) and fail to appreciate just how 'fearfully and wonderfully made' we are (Psalm 139:14).

One of the ways we can more fully enter into the story God has for us is to begin to better understand who we are and how God has made us. I'm a big fan of psychometric tools such as the Enneagram, StrengthsFinder, Myers-Briggs, the temperament colours and the list goes on! They are not meant to box us in or totally define us, but they are tools that can help us identify how we are uniquely made and then through our wiring, better get to know our Creator and the plans he has for us.

As well as encouraging you to check out the tools I mentioned above, let me mention one of the easiest to work with that has been inspired by *Sacred Pathways: Discover Your Soul's Path to God* by Gary Thomas.[36]

In it, Thomas names nine unique pathways he believes many of us exhibit. We can be more than one, of course, but they are helpful to us in identifying who we are and how we are made.

Let me take these great ideas and suggest seven pathways with a brief definition of each:

1. The relational pathway

An example might be the apostle Peter who always seemed to be around people. If this is your primary pathway, then solitude feels like a prison sentence to you and whenever you want to experience God, you want to do it with other people. When you interact with others, you feel God's presence more acutely. If that's you, lean into that, make sure you are building in time and space for life-giving relationships. A caution for you would be to beware of too many superficial relationships and not enough relationships that go deeper. A healthy stretch for you would be to develop some capacity for silence and self-reflection and maybe at times don't say everything that immediately comes into your mind!

2. The Intellectual pathway

An example might be the apostle Paul, considered by many to have possessed one of the greatest minds in history. If this is your primary pathway, you will draw close to God when you think, study and debate. At times you struggle to understand those who say they 'feel' God's presence or they 'sense' it; for you, your mind has to understand before your heart can feel it or sense it. To strengthen this for you, create time and space to study and be around others also wired this way. A caution would be to be careful not to get too judging of others who don't think to the extent you do. A stretch would be to enter into times of sung worship more and try some other creative worship expressions. Remember the goal is not to just to know your Creator but to love him!

3. The serving pathway

An example might be the character Dorcas who the Bible says was 'always doing good and helping' (Acts 9:36). If this is your primary pathway, you will love to help others and struggle to sit still for too long. You come alive when you serve; you don't have to be asked, you just dive right in, willing and eager to help. To strengthen this pathway for you, serve consistently, not just when the mood takes you. A caution would be to not resent others who don't have your pathway and remember you are always more than what you do. A stretch would be to balance serving with community along with rest and self-care. Learn to receive as well as to give, and use words as well as actions.

4. The worship pathway

An example might be King David, who as well as being a warrior and a leader was known for being a worshipper. If this is you, you love to sing, and when intellectuals are asking, 'When is the singing over?' you cry, 'Sing it again!' Worship music is your spiritual lifeblood and to strengthen that in you, make gathered worship a priority in your life. A caution for you would be to beware of judging others who are not as expressive as you. A stretch might also be to try some musical styles other than the ones you prefer, and also add study into your life so you can ground your experience in truth.

5. The activist pathway

An example might be Nehemiah, who rebuilt the city gates and walls. If this is your primary pathway, you have a passion and energy that others find both inspiring and intimidating. You love solving problems and you love getting things done, it's when you feel the most alive spiritually. To strengthen this, get stuck into something worthy and a challenge; maybe volunteer in church or in your community. A caution for you might be that at times you can have the tendency to run over people in your passion to get things done. Maybe slow down a little and ensure people are coming with you and not being left in your wake! A stretch would be to balance activism with solitude, to lean into being, not just doing.

6. The contemplative pathway

An example here might be Mary, the sister of Martha. If this is you, you love unstructured, uninterrupted time. Reflection comes naturally to you and you like your own company. You have a large capacity for prayer and lots of people drain you if you don't have space for just you and God. To strengthen this in you, give yourself permission to be alone and set time aside for that. As you connect with God in that space, he creates capacity within you for engaging with people and the world around you. A caution would be to avoid seeing retreat as an escape instead of dealing with issues or conflict in your life. A stretch would be to actively serve and intentionally connect with others.

7. The creation pathway

An example here might be Jesus! Yes, of course he is an example of all the pathways in ways no human being can ever attain to, but like Jesus, you feel closest to God when you are in creation. Nature and the outdoors replenishes and revitalises you, it restores your soul. To strengthen this, get outside often and schedule time for that. A caution would be the danger of escapism and in doing so forgetting that the pinnacle of creation is humankind, it's people. A stretch for you would be to stay relationally connected; maybe find others who are wired this way and experience creation together. It might also be good to ensure serving is on your radar also, as sometimes the ability to stoop low to serve connects us with the Creator the most; we are never more like God than when we serve.

So there it is, seven pathways that can help you discover your pathway to the Creator and in doing so, liberate you to play your part in his greater story.

For a link to a simple assessment tool which can help you identify yourself, head to the website of resources for The Playground via the QR code or web link.

As you discover your pathway, your wiring, your temperament and strengths, be careful to resist the urge to use them as excuses: 'I'm not wired that way', 'That's not me', etc. Instead, we lean into who we are but we also learn from others wired differently to us. A final comment: let's celebrate the diversity of one another; we are all so unique and that's the beauty of a Creator God who invites us each to play our part in his greater story.

My home

We are all 'fearfully and wonderfully made', created by a God who knows us, who loves us and who has a plan for us to play our part in his epic adventure story. That truth is also true for your home; whatever the make-up of your family or how you define it, God invites you into his story as a family.

I am so grateful to Care for the Family, not only for all they have done and are doing over many years to strengthen families, but for their willingness and openness to share resources with families and the wider Church. So, you could try these ideas on your own, or with whoever shares your home with you. If there are children in your home, get them together and dive into these amazing ideas from Care for the Family's Kitchen Table Project and remember, faith grows as you go![37]

As you go . . . to eat

Think about where your food comes from and pray for that place.

Ask a different member of your home to pray for your food at each meal time.

As you go . . . out

In the woods or local parks, look around you and talk about how unique and creative God is, and how he has made us unique too.

Before you go out in the car or on the bus, play the gratitude game: each member of the family thinks of one thing they are grateful for that day and says it out loud, *or* at the park, say one thing you're grateful for every time you go down the slide.

As you go . . . around the house

Have a praise party and let your children choose their favourite praise and worship songs.

While baking talk about how all the different ingredients come together to make something wonderful. When doing this, reference the way God has made creation come together to make something wonderful.

As you go . . . to bed

Chat about where you saw God at work that day.

Ask your child to think of one thing they saw that day that God created and be thankful for that.

As you go . . . to church

Write an encouragement card to give to someone in your church.

Discuss with your family or those you live with a way you could serve in church together. Maybe it's cooking a meal for someone or taking another family out for a picnic?

My church

When it comes to a response to the environmental challenges our world faces, it's often left to the ardent and passionate few to respond. What if every church in our nation took up the call to care for the planet that God has created? What if we individually and corporately did what we could do to ensure the story of our planet continues? The problem is, we often don't know where to start!

That's where other organisations and people can help us.

A Rocha UK is a Christian charity working to protect and restore the natural world and is committed to equipping Christians and churches in the UK to care for the environment.[38]

Use the QR code to check out their website and their countless resources. Why not encourage your church leadership to take some of the surveys that will help you assess where you are as a church and how you can respond?

There are also individuals like Ruth Valerio who have made available some excellent resources to help us all grow in this important area. Again, use the QR code to find out more.

Spend some time in prayer on your own or with others in your church, and if you aren't sure what to pray, use some of these statements A Rocha UK provide in their vision statement:

> The world we want to see:
>
> A world where stable climate and abundant nature, where oceans, rivers, air and soil are free of human pollution.
>
> Where human society lives in balance with the rest of nature . . .
>
> Where all people and communities have access to healthy nature locally
>
> Where the Church worldwide understands the biblical mandate to care for all of God's creation . . .
>
> And where, through Churches and Christians adopting a right relationship with the rest of Creation, others are drawn to a closer, life-giving relationship with our Creator God.[39]

PART TWO
Redeemer

Rescuer, Restorer, Saviour, Forgiver, Reconciler . . .

At the last
Hearts ached the peace was so consuming
Yet in the grass a snake was carousing
Perusing the garden of heaven
Seeking an ear to drip venom
An eye to become conceited
A mind that's indecisive
You couldn't Adam and Eve it
But God's love became unrequited
The invitations multiply
And we act like we're uninvited
Why else did David cry:
Give me a heart that's undivided.
Undecided, when faced with God's serenity
Responding to eternity
We gave him infidelity
In the testaments
Our pestilence became hereditary
The mind contorts
The lies distort
The last resort
A great divorce
There's too much acrimony
If the wages of sin are death
We're still paying alimony
How could the grave
Become our testimony
We pay respects
But we couldn't pay enough reparations
To cover the gap
Between this separation
In desperation, the cross seemed certain

As mourners assemble
Cries are curdling
And legs tremble
Under the weight of burden
But power was in the temple
Tearing away the curtain
From the hands of a serpent
What beauty
The Saviour, answering his call to duty
He didn't respawn
Jesus ain't playing *Call of Duty*
But the lines are redrawn
In the Potter's hands
Clay is reformed
Dead in our sins
In his arms we are reborn
Held by the gardener
Death supposed to be a hardener
Reconciled to sin's pardoner
Redemption just his starter
Drained the cup of judgement
Like he's drinking sharpeners
Joseph the carpenter
But the apprentice
Now sits as the master
A woman approaches
Carrying a jar of alabaster
Spirit is broken
She seeks a plaster
Son speaks a different language
The broken need more than a bandage
So an excuse became a confession

Then a profession of truth
Spoken without caution
To a prostitute
This orphan who lay there
Body forbidden
Arose as a daughter
Her sins forgiven
They who have ears to hear
Let them listen!

The
Classroom

For your Maker is your husband –
the Lord Almighty is his name –
the Holy One of Israel is your Redeemer;
he is called the God of all the earth.
The Lord will call you back
as if you were a wife deserted and distressed
in spirit –
a wife who married young,
only to be rejected,' says your God.
'For a brief moment I abandoned you,
but with deep compassion I will bring you back.
In a surge of anger
I hid my face from you for a moment,
but with everlasting kindness
I will have compassion on you,'
says the Lord your Redeemer.

(Isaiah 54:5-8)

O for a thousand tongues to sing
my great Redeemer's praise,
the glories of my God and King,
the triumphs of his grace!

(Charles Wesley)[40]

CHAPTER SIX

God in the Middle

We have been saying all through this book, everybody has a story and everybody's story matters. Nobody gets the story they really want, but here's the amazing truth: everybody's story can find redemption, meaning and purpose when it's part of a bigger story . . . a greater story.

What makes a great story, a great movie, a great play, a great drama? *Tension.*

The scene is set, the characters introduced and you start to get drawn in, but the moment tension is introduced, you're hooked. Whether it's when tragedy strikes, or there's a setback, a disaster, a threat or a betrayal, something creates the tension and the story now has meaning and gravitas, now it matters.

Isaiah saw tension all around him. The people of God began so well, thanks to their Creator God who perfectly established the world in order and his people within it. Yet as Isaiah looked around Judah in his day, the world was not as it should have been. The people had abandoned God and his values, social injustice was rife and now they found themselves in exile; judgement had fallen and with it we see a mirror into the human condition. Humanity began in a state of perfection and harmony with God and his creation, but through our own free will and choice we ended up in exile and in need of redemption. We often read (and sing) about redemption, but what does it actually mean?

A dictionary will often help us see redemption in the context of being saved from sin or evil. It will also usually suggest gaining possession back of something that has been lost or taken, and involved in this will be a payment of some kind.

Some of the words used in the Bible for redemption paint a more vivid picture for us:

> In him we have *redemption* through his blood, the forgiveness of sins, in accordance with the riches of God's grace . . .
>
> (Ephesians 1:7, emphasis mine)

The original word here is *apolutrusis,* which means 'release effected by payment of ransom'; it has a sense of buying back from someone, re-purchasing.

> Christ *redeemed* us from the curse of the law by becoming a curse for us, for it is written: 'Cursed is everyone who is hung on a pole.'
>
> (Galatians 3:13, emphasis mine)

The word here is *exagorazo,* which means 'to buy up or to rescue from loss'. The common understanding at the time was the idea of buying at the market place. Another dimension to this was a release from the power of another. All really common understandings in people's minds in ancient times.

This descriptive word suggests for us pictures of slaves being bought in the marketplace and then being released and given their freedom.

In Isaiah the primary word for redemption is *gaal*:

> But now, this is what the LORD says –
> he who created you, Jacob,
> he who formed you, Israel:
> 'Do not fear, for I have *redeemed* you;
> I have summoned you by name; you are mine.

(Isaiah 43:1, emphasis mine)

This word *gaal* means, 'to redeem by acting as a kinsman', which is the idea of a close relative, a next of kin.

Isaiah's original audience knew they needed redeeming, they knew they needed rescuing. They had fallen out of that original place of harmony with God and his creation and now found themselves a people in exile, bereft of home and hope. It was a far cry from the place they used to occupy ... it was quite a fall.

Speaking of a fall, that's the tension in their story and it's also the tension in our story. The doctrine of the 'Fall' is a major theme in the greater story of God. It originates in the first few chapters of the Bible in Genesis when God gives the first people, Adam and Eve, free will and dominion over everything with clear instructions to avoid sampling the fruit of one particular tree. Just to be clear, they had free reign to enjoy everything on offer apart from one thing and, of course, human nature is such that we go for the one thing we shouldn't rather than enjoy all the rest that we should. The tension in the story increases when Satan tempts Adam and Eve to disobey God, to believe a different voice, to trust a different story and because God gave them the ultimate loving gift, free will, they succumbed to that voice and with it the story took a dramatic and devastating turn. The voice they chose to believe meant they questioned the authority of God for the first time, 'Did God really say...?' (Genesis 3:1). It meant they doubted the goodness of God, the wisdom of God and the truth of God for the first time. As a result of their actions and choices, disconnection with God took place; sin, brokenness, pain, discord, injustice and ultimately death itself entered the story, it entered our story, but even in that moment of drama and tragedy, God was already working on rewriting the story.

Shortly after they ate the fruit they were told not to eat, their awareness of themselves changed; they became aware of shame and so they hid in the garden. It is here that the first question ever asked in the Bible takes place when God says, 'Where are you?' (v. 9).

First questions are important. If my wife asks to take my new car to the shops and I agree (which of course I do), then thirty minutes later she calls, saying, 'I have some bad news. I've been in a crash,' how important is my first question? What should that first question be? 'How's the car ... no ... how are you?' Our first question reveals a lot, and God's first question to Adam and Eve revealed a lot too. He wasn't asking them where they were because he didn't know, he was asking because he wanted them to locate themselves relationally with himself. His first question wasn't geographical, it was relational. God created us for relationship and it broke his heart when that relationship was broken because of the Fall. Interestingly, God came in the 'cool of the day' (v. 8) which is when he went for walks with Adam and Eve; this is such a tender revelation of the heart and posture of God, who seeks relationship so much more than religion. Immediately he sets in motion his plan for redemption. Yes, they have to leave the garden and now they are aware of their nakedness, but God provides animal skins to cover their shame and exposure, hinting at what is to come when a sacrifice will be made to cover our shame and exposure to sin. Even in judgement and consequence God is good and God is kind.

There's a concept in Jewish thought called *tikkun olam*, which means 'the repairing of the world'. Although it's not found in biblical writings, it's an aspirational thought echoed in the pages of Isaiah and across the whole story of God. God is on a quest to redeem and restore, to recover and rebuild, and he invites you and me to join him in that epic adventure. The film *Schindler's List* is a moving and powerful story of Oscar Schindler, a German industrialist who risks his life to help Jews escape the clutches of the Nazi regime in the Second World War. In the film one of the most memorable scenes is when one of the characters quotes the saying from the Jewish Scriptures: 'Whoever saves one life saves the world entire.'[41] This is paraphrased from the Talmud, Mishnah Sanhedrin 37a.

Isaiah sees something of God's plan for redemption, but for us to really grasp this, we need to grapple with understanding that there are various layers of meaning often contained in biblical texts and stories. What do I mean? Jewish rabbinic interpretation was often based on what they called the four levels:

P'shat – straight, direct, literal, the most obvious meaning of the text

Remez – hinted at, implied, maybe allegorical, meaning behind the obvious

D'rash – Inquire, seek, going even deeper into meaning

Sod – secret, mysterious, reserved for God himself to really know and understand[42]

Without getting too hung up on this, it is interesting to consider when we come to explore the richness and depth of Isaiah's discourse around redemption. An example of this is when we come to look at the idea of the suffering servant, such a major theme in Isaiah's story and writings. He begins with judgement and lots of woes, but from chapter 40 onwards the tone changes as he introduces the idea of redemption around the concept of the 'servant'.

In chapters 40 to 54 we see the 'servant' mentioned time after time. It is the servant discourse that starts with the word 'comfort' and ushers in hope.

> But you, Israel, my *servant*, Jacob, whom I have chosen, you descendants of Abraham my friend . . .
>
> (Isaiah 41:8, emphasis mine)

> 'You are my witnesses,' declares the LORD, 'and my *servant* whom I have chosen . . .'
>
> (Isaiah 43:10a, emphasis mine)

> But now listen, Jacob, my *servant*, Israel, whom I have chosen.
>
> (Isaiah 44:1, emphasis mine)

In each of the references to 'servant' it's the same original word, *ebed*, and it means a slave or a bondservant. Our modern frame of reference doesn't help us understand the full meaning here because in the ancient world, slavery was commonplace and an accepted practice. The notion of a bondservant has rich meaning, as it not only features early on in the Old Testament but is the idea Paul uses when he refers to himself as a *doulos* or a 'bondservant' (Romans 1:1, NKJV). There was an ancient practice whereby the bondservant may be given their freedom but they could choose to stay to serve their master, not because they had to but because they wanted to.

In our modern world, even the concept of servant is one we find difficult to embrace; after all, nobody minds being a servant till they get treated like one, right?

Who is the 'servant' Isaiah is referring to here?

By the time we get to Isaiah 53 (and we will get there) we are all screaming, 'It's Jesus!' and in so many ways it is. But let's not miss something really important here.

When Isaiah refers to 'servant' he could be referring to many things. He could be referring to the people of God, to a portion of the people of God (a remnant), or even to individuals that God will use to bring about his purposes, even ungodly kings like Cyrus or Darius. This is where the many layers of meaning in Scripture come into their own, a literal meaning that meant something at the time, a hinted at meaning that may only be apparent if you have eyes to see or ears to hear, and even a prophetic 'to come' meaning. All are valid and all speak to the central idea of redemption: *for God to put right what has been damaged and destroyed, it will require a servant.*

So, when he so beautifully and powerfully opens up the idea of a suffering servant in Isaiah 53, could there also be a sense in which God is calling his people to a display of suffering and perseverance that in itself could be redemptive for the world? Could we the Church be an agent of redemption in and for the world, but only as we suffer and as we serve? Might it be that what God is looking for in our churches is not churches that strive to be the best church *in* their community but instead the best church *for* their community? We will explore what this could and should look like as we move out of the classroom into the living room and eventually the playground.

If we look at Scripture through these layers of meaning, it opens up a greater story in which you and I find identity, meaning and purpose. With this in mind, let's now turn our attention to where we do see Jesus in the pages of Isaiah.

Therefore the Lord himself will give you a sign: the virgin will conceive and give birth to a son, and will call him Immanuel.

(Isaiah 7:14)

The context of these words is that King Ahaz has rejected the clear word of the Lord, and he will be given a sign that he cannot fully understand. A woman will become pregnant, and this sign carries with it both a promise and a threat. There is literal fulfilment for Ahaz in his context, but of course it also speaks of what or rather who will come . . . Messiah.

As John Watts says in his commentary on Isaiah:

Thus the announcement of God's sign to Ahaz in his hour of despair is a fitting reference to illuminate the birth of a lowly infant in stable straw to whom God has destined to save the world not by force of arms but by meek acceptance of humiliation and death . . .[43]

There's so much more:

The people walking in darkness
have seen a great light;
on those living in the land of deep darkness
a light has dawned.

(Isaiah 9:2)

Light is a key recurring image in Scripture and plays out heavily in the writings of Isaiah.

It was light that ushered in the formation of the universe when God said, 'Let there be light' (Genesis 1:3). It was the fall of an archangel often referred to as 'an angel of light' (2 Corinthians 11:14) that we read about in Isaiah 14:

How you have fallen from heaven,
morning star, son of the dawn!
You have been cast down to the earth,
you who once laid low the nations!

(Isaiah 14:12)

Whether this is a direct reference to Satan or not, the fall plunged the world into darkness that we still experience in so many ways. Light is revealing, light is warming, light is energising, light is replenishing and the servant referred to time and time again in Isaiah is the one who will bring light.

Then we really start to think in Christmas mode as we read these amazing words:

For to us a child is born,
to us a son is given,
and the government will be on
his shoulders.
And he will be called
Wonderful Counsellor, Mighty God,
Everlasting Father, Prince of Peace.

(Isaiah 9:6)

With the declaration of light at the end of their tunnel, Isaiah then pivots to hope as he points to a future better than the present or even the past.

Alex Motyer in his commentary on Isaiah puts it this way:

This hope is sure. 9 v.1-7 is couched in past tenses; the future is written as something which has already happened, for it belonged to the prophetic consciousness of men like Isaiah to cast themselves forward in time and then look back at the mighty acts of God, saying to us: Look forward to it, it is certain, he has already done it! . . . those walking in darkness can see the light ahead and are sustained by hope.'[44]

Let's pause and ponder these four magnificent statements that remind us of why Jesus is *greater* and why there is no servant, no redeemer like him.

He is a Wonderful Counsellor – he is wisdom when you need it the most

The original word in Hebrew here for wonderful is the word *pele*. I can't help thinking of the Brazilian footballer who at the age of seventeen lit up the world with his electrifying football skills and went on to become one of the greatest players of all time. He was called by many commentators and fans as out of this world, extraordinary, astounding, and yet he was still very human. When Isaiah uses this word *pele* about the Messiah that is to come, it also means 'out of this world, extraordinary, astounding, almost supernatural'. Here's the thing: when you come to God through Jesus for wisdom, for advice, what you get is supernatural, astounding, extraordinary, out of this world. Yes, by all means go to other people for wisdom and advice, but never forget the best wisdom comes from above as James, the brother of Jesus, puts it in his letter to the early Church: 'If any of you lacks wisdom, you should ask God, who gives generously to all without finding fault, and it will be given to you' (James 1:5).

This is an aspect of the character of our redeemer. He is wisdom when you need it most, but he is also more than that ...

He is the Mighty God – he is strength when yours is running out

The word for mighty used here is *gibbor* and refers to a champion, a warrior of extraordinary strength who stands head and shoulders above every other would-be champion.

Our redeemer, Jesus, is not just a little bit stronger than others, he is not just an upgrade on others, he is in a totally different league, a category all of his own. When you come to him and make him your Lord and leader, you have access to all the fullness of God. As the apostle Paul puts it in his letter to the Colossian church: 'For God was pleased to have all his fullness dwell in him' (Colossians 1:19). He is strength when yours is running out, but there's still more:

He is the Everlasting Father – he is security when life feels unstable

In the original language, these two words are just one word, and it's the concept of eternity. He is perpetually our Father, he is eternally our Father, he is without end, always our Father. I had an amazing dad but he was human, his strength ran out, his patience ran out, his love sometimes ran out, but not so with our heavenly Father. He is security when life feels unstable – and still there's more:

He is the Prince of Peace – he brings calm when you sense you might be sinking

The word here for 'peace' is the beautiful Hebrew word *shalom*. It's a word that's difficult to fully translate or understand, but it contains within it the idea of completeness, wholeness, wellbeing, flourishing, goodness, rightness, a sense of being well with our soul, with our fellow man, with our God and with our world. Don't we need *shalom* more these days than ever?

- Why not pause and consider these four aspects of the character of our redeemer? What do they mean to you? How might you draw them as a picture or use them to compose a poem?

There's still more to learn in the classroom ... let's take a deeper dive into chapter 53, but we must set it in its proper context, which means bringing in the last few verses of the previous chapter:

> See, my servant will act wisely;
> he will be raised and lifted up and highly exalted.
> Just as there were many who were appalled at him –
> his appearance was so disfigured beyond that of any human being
> and his form marred beyond human likeness –
> so he will sprinkle many nations,
> and kings will shut their mouths because of him.
> For what they were not told, they will see,
> and what they have not heard, they will understand. . . .
> He grew up before him like a tender shoot,
> and like a root out of dry ground.
> He had no beauty or majesty to attract us to him,
> nothing in his appearance that we should desire him.
> He was despised and rejected by mankind,
> a man of suffering, and familiar with pain.
> Like one from whom people hide their faces
> he was despised, and we held him in low esteem.
> Surely he took up our pain
> and bore our suffering,
> yet we considered him punished by God,
> stricken by him, and afflicted.
> But he was pierced for our transgressions,
> he was crushed for our iniquities;
> the punishment that brought us peace was on him,
> and by his wounds we are healed.

(Isaiah 52:13-15; 53:2-5)

Seen in context we see the fourth and final servant song in Isaiah. There are five stanzas in this song that beautifully portray the majesty of the servant of God, and how countercultural to our view of leadership and power this servant actually is. Stanza 1 (chapter 52:13-15) gives us almost a summary of the servant who we see as God's wisdom revealed. Stanza 2 (chapter 53:1-3), we see this servant as both despised and rejected. It's almost as if the more he grew, the less attractive he became and the more ordinary he appeared to many. Pierced and crushed point to the visceral nature of his sacrifice and death, as if to emphasise this is a suffering servant not a celebrity servant. Stanza 3 (chapter 53:4-6) shifts the focus from what he has done to what he has accomplished for others; he has taken up our pain, suffering and punishment so that we could be healed and find freedom, or putting it another way . . . redemption.

Within these verses is the concept of substitution, which is the idea that because God is holy and just, there must be retribution for wrong, there must be justice.

John Stott put it this way in his book *The Cross of Christ*: 'The only way for God's holy love to be satisfied is for his holiness to be directed in judgment upon his appointed substitute, in order that his love may be directed towards us in forgiveness . . .'[45] The New Testament puts it this way: 'God put the wrong on him who never did anything wrong, so we could be put right with God' (2 Corinthians 5:21, *The Message*).

The debt that was in our account caused by our sin and brokenness was shifted onto him, all of it, past, present and future. The enemy, the one the Bible calls the 'accuser' (Revelation 12:10), wants to shift it all back. He is always trying to place guilt and shame back onto our shoulders when God placed it all on the shoulders of his Son, the suffering servant, Jesus. His primary weapon is a voice, as it was in the Garden of

Eden and it still is, suggesting we believe another narrative and succumb to another story. God accomplished this redemptive work on the cross but confirmed it at the empty tomb; the 'It is finished' (John 19:30) Jesus cried from the cross was given a resounding 'Amen' when Jesus rose from the dead.

It gets even better because God then shifts the credit that is in Jesus' account into our account; this is called 'grace'. Jesus gets what we deserve and we get what Jesus deserved!

God made him who had no sin to be sin for us, so that in him we might become the righteousness of God.

(2 Corinthians 5:21)

This is the centrepiece of the greater story of God, this is what Isaiah saw not only in front of him in context but ahead of him prophetically. He looked through time to see the ultimate suffering servant who would bring about redemption and with it light and hope, the good news.

Stanza 4 (chapter 53:7-9) describes how this servant accomplished this great act of substitution and thus redemption. He did it silently, he did it painfully, he did it intentionally, he did it purposefully, he did it sacrificially. He did it for me and he did it for you ... there is no one *greater*.

Stanza 5 (chapter 53:10-12) we see the reward that comes to the servant, and the language here is reminiscent of the vision Isaiah saw in the year King Uzziah died; he sees the Lord 'high and lifted up (Isaiah 6:1, NKJV). Dishonour is turned to honour, weakness is turned to strength, defeat is turned to victory and the despised and rejected become the one given the highest place.

'Man of Sorrows,' what a name
For the Son of God who came
Ruined sinners to reclaim!
Hallelujah! what a Saviour!

Bearing shame and scoffing rude,
In my place condemned he stood;
Sealed my pardon with his blood:
Hallelujah! what a Saviour!

Guilty, vile, and helpless, we,
Spotless Lamb of God was he;
Full redemption – can it be?
Hallelujah! what a Saviour!

Lifted up was he to die,
'It is finished!' was his cry;
Now in heaven exalted high;
Hallelujah! what a Saviour!

When he comes, our glorious King,
To his kingdom us to bring,
Then anew this song we'll sing
Hallelujah! what a Saviour!

(Philip Bliss)[46]

There is one more reference to Jesus we must pay attention to, and that's found in Isaiah 61. This is so pivotal for our understanding of redemption in the greater story of God. These are the verses Jesus chooses to read out in the temple at the start of his earthly ministry. We read the account in Luke's Gospel chapter 4, and as you read these words, try to picture the tension in this scene as Jesus unfolds the ancient scroll and begins to read:

The Spirit of the Lord is on me,
because he has anointed me
to proclaim good news to the poor.
He has sent me to proclaim freedom for the prisoners
and recovery of sight for the blind,
to set the oppressed free,
to proclaim the year of the Lord's favour.

(Luke 4:18-19)

Then he rolled the scroll up and said, 'Today this scripture is fulfilled in your hearing' (v. 21).

Wow, talk about a mic-drop moment!

Everyone who listened knew the verses he was quoting were from the book of Isaiah and they knew with it came the overtones of the Messiah, the bringer of redemption to the story. Let's look at each phrase and with it, begin to open up how God has brought, does bring and will bring redemption to our lives and to our world.

Jesus chooses this passage to declare his manifesto, his mandate as the Messiah, and it is to bring good news to the poor. This phrase 'good news' or 'gospel' was a common one in the ancient world. The Greek term is *euangelion* and it's really important we grapple with this term as its meaning is so rich. Every ancient ruler had a *euangelion* – it is the announcement of a king and a kingdom. It's also the root of the word 'gospel' which means 'good news'. When a king is victorious in battle, a herald spreads the 'gospel', the 'good news', the *euangelion* that the king and his kingdom are still in control, or have arrived on the scene. In this moment Jesus announces that a new 'gospel' a new 'good news', a new *euangelion*, a new way of life has arrived, the kingdom of God.

It's a gospel of good news to the poor, the downtrodden, the disheartened, the disenfranchised. We must also remember that we can be 'poor' in all kinds of ways, not just materially; we can be poor relationally, morally, aspirationally, spiritually. In the Isaiah verses Jesus draws on, it says this 'gospel' will 'bind up the broken-hearted' (Isaiah 61:1). This implies the personal nature of God's presence and kingdom that will bring soothing, comfort, healing and wholeness. The word 'heart' is such a versatile word, as it covers all forms of human breakdown that damage our hearts. When Jesus says 'freedom for the prisoners', he is referring to Jubilee, that ancient practice whereby every fiftieth year people are set free from debts, property is restored and those living in slavery are released into freedom. This is the gospel, this is the good news, this is the *euangelion* that brings about redemption. 'Recovery of sight for the blind', 'release from darkness' (Isaiah 61:1), powerful phrases that paint a vivid picture of God's kingdom that brings light and hope where there is darkness and despair. As an aside, the word used here in Isaiah for 'release' means 'wide opening' and is only used here in this verse. The kind of redemption in God's greater story is a wider release than anything we can envisage. It's way more than forgiveness of sins so we go to heaven when we die. It's way more than access to a certain way of life and living that we may deem 'good' or even 'godly'. In fact, it is life as God intended, human flourishing; it's what it means to be fully human sustained and empowered by the breath and energy of God. It's a world where we are living for the fulfilment of what Jesus taught his followers to pray, 'your kingdom come, your will be done, on earth as it is in heaven' (Matthew 6:10).

Alec Motyer in his commentary on Isaiah says this: 'The *good news* embraces personal renewal and restoration(*bind up the broken-hearted*), release from restrictions imposed by people ... and the rectification of circumstances (*release ... for the prisoners*).'[47]

As Isaiah looks up, he sees the Lord; as he looks back, he sees a God who was at the beginning the Creator of the universe. Then he looks forward, and as he does, sees a God who is now in the middle, the God of redemption. He sees a God who sends his suffering servant to demonstrate a different and better way to use power and who ushers in a new *euangelion*, a new 'gospel' a new 'good news' to all humankind.

Now it's time to leave the classroom again and head back to the living room where we so often find ourselves in the middle of our story . . .

The
Living Room

CHAPTER SEVEN

Greater Than Our Mess

Yet you, LORD, are our Father.
We are the clay, you are the potter;
We are all the work of your hand.

(Isaiah 64:8)

God is at work in the mess. That's the message of the
Bible. That's why the Bible is not pretty. That's why
it's grimy, because God is working in the mess. He's
working in the tears.

(Matt Chandler)[48]

If there's one thing I know about you it's this, 'You're a mess.'
There, I've said it, and before you shut the book, let me explain.
I know you're a mess because I'm one. In fact, it's the one
thing that brings us all together, mess. We all have mess in our
lives, family mess, financial mess, relational mess. Some of us
are between messes, some of us are trying to sort out messes
(we call them teenagers!) and some of us are one decision
away from another mess. Some of us created and made our
own mess, some of us are the victims of the mess others have
created. Good news, the story of God is a story of hope for
people in a mess. The Creator is also the redeemer, and he

loves nothing more than mess because it attracts him, it draws him, it almost calls to him. You could put it this way: *The mess that brings us together is the mess that brought God near.*

As Isaiah's discourse develops from woes and judgement to hope and redemption, he repeats the idea of the 'day of favour' when God redeems and restores our messes, those intentional and those that were consequential because of the Fall.

God is greater than our mess

One of the key themes in Isaiah is light. Perhaps the most famous example is Isaiah 60:

> Arise, shine, for your light has come,
> and the glory of the LORD rises upon you.
> See, darkness covers the earth
> and thick darkness is over the peoples,
> but the LORD rises upon you
> and his glory appears over you.
> Nations will come to your light,
> and kings to the brightness of your dawn.
>
> (Isaiah 60:1-3)

When Jesus read from Isaiah 61 declaring the manifesto of the kingdom, he spoke about the 'year of the Lord's favour' and light being an essential component of that. When we find ourselves in mess, it's hard to see the light. Yet as Jesus moved around his world, he encountered so many people in so many messes and each time he brought some light into their darkness. The woman caught in the act of adultery in John 8, the dishonest tax collector in Luke 19, the woman at the well in John 4 and the dying thief on the cross in Luke 23. All of them in the darkness of their mess, sexual, material, relational, criminal, and yet to each person Jesus brought good news and he brought light.

You may not have followed Jesus into your mess, but you can follow him out of it

This is the good news of the gospel, the *euangelion* of God, the mess that brings us together is the mess that brought God near in Jesus. This is not only a message for us, it's a message entrusted to us for our communities and our world.

What about the mess we won't address?

A few years ago, while on a trip to Israel we stopped at the pool of Bethesda. I've already referred to this earlier when we sang in the church, but outside the church is the scene of one of Jesus' greatest and most perplexing miracles. We read of it in John 5 where Jesus encounters a common scene at this location, hundreds of people waiting to get into the water so they can receive their healing. There is all kind of imagery and layers of meaning around the scene; five covered colonnades, possibly a reference to the five books of the law called the Torah. Jesus encounters a man disabled for thirty-eight years, maybe referencing the thirty-eight years the children of Israel were in the wilderness before they prepared to go into the promised land. All of that is interesting but the most interesting part of this story is the question Jesus asks the man in verse 6: 'Do you want to get well?'

Imagine the guy's possible response to that question: 'Jesus, are you serious? How insensitive, how unfeeling, how cruel! I've been in this mess for thirty-eight years and you ask do I want to get well? Why would you even think that, let alone ask it?'

For a moment, don't focus on the physical situation this man is in, but ask yourself: is Jesus delving deeper into this man's mess? Why does Jesus often ask this or a similar question? Could it be that he is trying to ascertain if we really do want to change, if we really do want to get out of our mess, or could it be that he knows there is a mess in some of our lives we just won't address?

Many years ago, I read a book that focused on medical research especially relating to heart disease. (I know, I need to get out more!) The research focused on people who were told by doctors that unless they altered their lifestyle, they would die due to heart disease. Amazingly enough, only 1:7 made the changes.[49] Did that mean the other six wanted to die, or was there something deeper going on? We often say we want to address our mess, but there's something else at work within us that fights against that wish. It's like an accelerator and a brake that we apply at the same time. The apostle Paul puts it well: 'I do not understand what I do. For what I want to do I do not do, but what I hate I do' (Romans 7:15).

Here's the truth I know lives in me and, if I can suggest, also lives in you. Often we acknowledge our mess, say we want to change it but then do or don't do things that work against what we say we want. I say I want to lose weight but then I eat the wrong food at the wrong time, and yet I want to lose weight; why is that? Could it be that there's an underlying driver that's bigger for me than my desire to lose weight? Maybe food brings comfort, maybe my background taught me to eat when I can because I may not know where the next meal will come from? Whatever the reason is or whatever the mess is, the real reason we won't address our mess is often what lies beneath that. That's what Jesus is getting at with this man. Maybe he has got adjusted and accustomed to his situation; maybe a change would mean a new world and a new way of living? Maybe he would rather live in the mess he knows than step into the life he says he wants? Isn't that sometimes true of us too?

When we were at that pool of Bethesda, I spoke about this story, highlighting the fact that we all have a mess we won't address, and at the end of the talk a lady came to me from the group and shared her story. Her son was a drug addict and had tried many times to get out of the mess, but each time whatever was underlying in his life was greater than his desire to get out of the mess. In that place she came to the conclusion that he didn't want to address his mess enough and that broke her heart. There, by the ruins of the pool, she wept and asked me to pray for her son that somehow the light of Jesus would shine into her son's heart and he would address the mess that was holding him in chains. As we finished praying, I couldn't help but think how many of us also have mess that we won't address.

Speaking of mess, let me tell you Simon's story. It was the first Sunday of 2005. Just a few days earlier, on New Year's Day, Simon found himself waking up in a prison cell. The previous night had been a blur of drink and drugs, resulting in a violent act that he committed, which was to alter the course of his life. His parents drove him to our town where his grandmother lived, and they left him there exasperated, at a loss to know what to do with him; it was a mess. On the first Sunday in January, Simon left his grandmother's house with the thought of taking his own life, but instead found his way to our church. He heard the music and the singing but couldn't face people, so found a side room to sit in for the duration of the service. That Sunday I was speaking and Simon heard the words, 'It doesn't matter what you've done, what mess your life is in, there is always hope for a new start with God.' Those words resonated and the following week he came back and surrendered his life, mess and all, to Jesus. Over the next few weeks and months, we watched his faith grow and then came the moment he had to go to prison for what he had done. He often says, 'Most people leave prison to find freedom. I found freedom then went to prison!' After prison he continued to grow, eventually joining our staff team, where he led many people into a relationship with Jesus; they found redemption from their mess just as he had. He met a woman, they married and had two girls along with two previous daughters Simon already had from a previous relationship. During COVID-19, Simon was asked to plant a church in the city of Wolverhampton, and that church is growing as a beacon of light and hope, helping others who find themselves in all types of messes find redemption and a new story for their lives.

Our mess may not look like Simon's mess, but when we find ourselves in a mess, how do we find our way out, and in doing so, discover a God who is greater than our mess? The repeating announcement you hear on the tube station isn't a bad place to start:

See it – Say it – Sorted

See it

This is about bringing things into the light, seeing the mess for what it really is and stop excusing, defending or justifying. A critical component to this is self-awareness, that often elusive ability to really know yourself. The sad truth is we all have blind spots, and if you are saying to yourself as you are reading this, 'I don't have any blind spots,' then that's your blind spot right there! By definition, we cannot see them, and these are often at the heart of some of the messes we find ourselves getting into. In the 1950s, the psychologists Joseph Luft and Harrington Ingham developed a framework for understanding ourselves known as the Johari Window (google it!).[50]

In this tool there are four quadrants of existence; the known to self and known to others, the not known to self but known to others, the known to self but not known to others and the unknown to self and others. The goal for human flourishing and a way to minimise the messes we get ourselves into would be to see as much as we can within ourselves brought into the 'known to self and others' quadrant. The Bible might call it 'bringing things into the light' (see Ephesians 5:13) and since 'all truth is God's truth' we need not fear these kinds of tools and frameworks, as they can help us see ourselves and thus better understand God and his relationship to us as his created beings. Tim Keller put it this way based on a famous quote by the theologian John Calvin, 'We cannot know God without knowing ourselves and we cannot know ourselves without knowing God.'[51]

The Johari Window has pioneered the way for other helpful tools in this area such as StrengthsFinder, the Enneagram, Myers-Briggs and many more.

Say it

This is about naming it, preferably to someone appropriate who can hold you accountable. The Bible is clear about the connection between confession (speaking things out loud to God and at times to others) and freedom. James puts it this way: 'Therefore confess your sins to each other and pray for each other so that you may be healed' (James 5:16).

We cannot tame what we will not name.

We can receive forgiveness from God directly, but there's a freedom that can come through appropriate confession. Notice I use the word 'appropriate'; you see, we can often express our pain these days through social media, which may feel cathartic at the time but isn't that helpful for us or for others. I'm sure there are those God has placed in or around your life who would be safe to share aspects of your 'mess'; after all, not everybody needs to know everything going on in you, but when you find the right people, there's healing in that as you begin to 'say it'.

However, saying it still isn't enough; we need to move to the third stage, which I want to suggest isn't 'sorted' because there's still work to be done.

Sort it

This is about taking responsibility, getting help if needed, bringing it to Jesus, who can do what we cannot do, who can make possible what we only see as impossible, and inviting others into our mess who can bring help, accountability and support. There may not be immediate change or breakthrough, but through persistence we can see that mess addressed and find the life we were created to live.

Having said all of this, we can also find ourselves in a mess that we cannot address even if we wanted to. A mess that is beyond our understanding, beyond our capabilities and here again, God proves he is greater because he brings the one gift we seek the most in the middle of that type of mess . . . peace.

The most common Greek word for 'peace' in the New Testament is the word *eirene* which means 'rest, wholeness, health'. Its Hebrew equivalent is the word *shalom*, a central theme in the *euangelion*, the good news of the gospel of the kingdom. Just before Jesus went to the cross, he gave his followers a promise of peace: 'I am leaving you with a gift – peace of mind and heart. And the peace I give is a gift the world cannot give. So don't be troubled or afraid' (John 14:27, NLT).

They then find themselves in the middle of the ultimate mess – Jesus is dead and buried and all hope seems gone, the story seems over. Then Jesus appears to these same followers after his resurrection, and the very first thing He says is, 'Peace be with you!' (John 20:19).

I don't know what mess you find yourself in at the moment. I do know the mess that brings us together also brought Jesus near. I do know that if we will address what mess we can address, Jesus will be right there with us doing what we cannot do. I do know that if we are not able to address the mess, Jesus promises his peace right in the middle.

> ## *We are all in the middle of our story and that's where we find Jesus . . . in the middle.*

I've found peace far beyond all understanding
Let it flow when my mind's under siege
All anxiety bows in the presence
Of Jesus the keeper of peace
And peace is a promise he keeps.[52]

- What mess do you currently find yourself in?

- Is it something you need to address or is there a peace you need to receive?

Prayer for when you find yourself in a mess

Lord, I stand before you in the middle of a mess.
For my part in the mess, I confess it and ask for your forgiveness.
For my actions and reactions that have added to the mess I am truly sorry.
For the part of the mess I had no control over that has been so damaging, I ask for your help.

I choose to address the mess even if it costs.
I choose to receive your peace in the middle of the mess.
For you are greater than my mess.

Amen

CHAPTER EIGHT

Greater Than Our Pain

But the fact is, it was *our* pains he carried . . .

(Isaiah 53:4, *The Message*)

We can ignore even pleasure. But pain insists upon
being attended to. God whispers to us in our pleasures,
speaks in our conscience, but shouts in our pains: it is
his megaphone to rouse a deaf world.

(C.S. Lewis)[53]

What's your earliest memory of pain? Mine was being pushed
around on my small bike by the older girls in the street (it
was the start of things to come!). All was going well until
one of the girls got a bit carried away and I lost control. The
next thing I remember was hurtling headlong into a wall, the
crash only being broken by my face against said wall. My lip
exploded with blood (yes, I can be a bit dramatic) and then I
found myself standing at our front door banging loudly hoping
and praying Mum was in.

Pain comes in all kinds of shapes and sizes

From physical pain that many have to bear day in day out, to the relational pain of betrayal, rejection, abandonment and death. Then there's the emotional and mental pain of disappointment, failure and setback. There's the pain of unrequited love and the pain of a dream that's appearing to die. When it comes to pain, we are often caught out by the comparison game, either, 'My pain is bigger than your pain,' or 'What right have I got to be in pain compared to your pain?'

My wife was trained as a nurse and in those days (Florence Nightingale era!) there was a saying, 'pain is what the patient says it is', which I think is actually quite helpful because let's face it, pain is pain and no matter what pain it is, it's ... well ... painful.

When it comes to pain, we all have a problem thinking about God

To some, pain is the proof that God doesn't exist: 'How could a loving God let this happen?' Funny, people who say they don't believe in God talk about God a lot when bad things happen; surely you can't blame a God who doesn't exist, but then who do you blame? To others, pain is a conundrum when they think about a God they believe exists, but if God exists, he is either bad (allows it to happen), or weak (he can't do anything about it).

The Greek philosopher Epicurus expressed some of this in his now famous trilemma:[54]

> If God is unable to prevent evil, then he is not all powerful
> If God is not willing to prevent evil then he is not all good
> If God is both willing and able to prevent evil, why does evil exist?

We could substitute or add in the word 'pain' when he talks about evil, and we see the problem many of us have when it comes to pain. I think we express it a little more viscerally than Epicurus did. I suggested earlier that Isaiah must have thought along these lines as he looked at the pain around him, surely crying out as we often do, *'God, are you there? God, do you care? God, can you do anything about this?'*

Isaiah knew about pain, the pain of loss when his mentor and king Uzziah died. The pain of seeing his nation in exile, the pain of longing for a better future for his nation. When you find yourself in pain, it's hard to see the story and how God is working that story out; the bigger picture is eclipsed by the present pain. The good news of the story of God is that God is greater than our pain. The God who created us and redeemed us is greater than the pain that threatens to consume us.

Many Christians become disillusioned with faith when pain comes, but actually isn't it true that you only become disillusioned if you have illusions in the first place?

The greater story of God should never include illusions; it doesn't have to, Jesus was crystal clear: 'I have told you these things, so that in me you may have peace. In this world you will have trouble. But take heart! I have overcome the world' (John 16:33).

Jesus was always clear, to be human is to experience pain and centuries later the band R.E.M. reiterated that truth with the song, 'Everybody Hurts'.[55] Just as that is a fact, so is the fact Jesus goes on to say, '...take heart! I have overcome the world.' In other words, 'You've no need to despair, *I am greater than your pain.'*

So how do we know that God is greater than our pain? How do we experience a God who is there, who does care and can do something about our pain?

Isaiah develops this beautiful picture of the suffering servant in chapter 53, which we have considered in the classroom, but how does this play out in the living room when it's not theory we need but reality? The often repeated preacher story comes to mind here, of when a small child who was afraid of the dark called out one night to her mother for reassurance. Her loving parent said, 'It's OK, God will be with you, go back to sleep.' The little girl said, 'But Mummy, I need a God with skin on!' When we are in pain, when we find ourselves in the middle of our story and we have no idea how it will turn out, it's not a concept of God we need but a 'God with skin on'. That is exactly what I believe Isaiah had in mind when he spoke of the suffering servant who was to come.

Let's take some time to reflect on how the suffering servant handled his pain, and what that means for us and our pain. On the night before Jesus went to the cross, we read the intensity and reality of the pain he was carrying:

> They went to a place called Gethsemane, and Jesus said to his disciples, 'Sit here while I pray.' He took Peter, James and John along with him, and he began to be deeply distressed and troubled. 'My soul is <u>overwhelmed with sorrow to the point of death,</u>' he said to them. 'Stay here and keep watch.'
>
> (Mark 14:32-34)

He was carrying intense pain, relational, mental, emotional, physical and spiritual which we see as the story continues:

> Going a little farther, he fell to the ground and prayed that if possible the hour might pass from him. '*Abba*, Father,' he said, 'everything is possible for you. Take this cup from me. Yet not what I will, but what you will.'
>
> (Mark 14:35-36)

Jesus is asking his Father the same questions you and I ask, *'God, are you there? God, do you care? God, can you do anything about this?'*

So, what did God the Father do? He swept down from heaven and miraculously took all the pain away. Instead of going to the cross, God found a more comfortable, palatable route for Jesus to go, thus proving to us all that the way of the cross is pain free! Is that what he did? NO! He didn't answer Jesus' prayer in the way he wanted it answered; have you ever thought about that? Jesus himself had to contend with unanswered prayer – this is so big if we let it impact us. Jesus himself did not get the answer to his prayer that he asked for or so desperately wanted. That's huge and should be an encouragement to us when our prayers don't seem to be answered the way we want or expect. If God the Father didn't answer the prayers of his Son in the way he wanted, what did he do instead?

> An angel from heaven appeared to him and strengthened him. And being in anguish, he prayed more earnestly, and his sweat was like drops of blood falling to the ground.
> (Luke 22:43-44)

God didn't take the pain away but God met him in the pain, the angel came and strengthened him.

Jesus is greater than our pain because he has carried our pain. You and I can't point the finger at God and say he doesn't know what pain feels like, because he does, and if Jesus himself was strengthened in his pain, we can also be strengthened in ours. People often ask the question, 'Why do bad things happen to good people?' I get that, I really do, but who determines 'good' anyway? It's relative and comparative and actually none of us are 'good' in comparison to God. In fact, something 'bad' has only ever happened to someone truly 'good' once in all of human history and that someone was Jesus.

So, when we do carry pain, what do we do with it? How do we experience a God who is *greater* than our pain in the middle of our pain and in the middle of our story?

Let me suggest a few things ...

When you're in pain, don't pull out of life

The temptation to withdraw is a common one, but when we do that, we lose connection with the source of our comfort and strength. Early on in my leadership of our church, a young girl died in her mother's arms due to a freak asthma attack. It was my first child funeral in such tragic circumstances and I remember the weeks and months afterwards talking, praying, crying with the family. Then I remember when they came back to church and it was at the time we were all singing the song, 'Blessed Be Your Name'. The bridge section talks about what God gives and what he takes away, such difficult words for those parents to sing; in fact, I remember the mother saying to me, 'I can't sing those words right now; actually, I can't sing any words at all.' Then she said these words that I will never forget, 'I can't sing but I can stand in the way of God, that's all I can do right now, stand in the way of God.'

When you are in pain, don't pull out of life, don't pull out of community and if you cry that's OK, if you can't sing that's OK, just stand in the way of God. He is *greater than your pain.*

There's something else we should be aware of ...

When you're in pain, don't transfer the pain

An aspect that often accompanies pain is grief. Whether
the pain is caused by the death of a loved one, the end of a
relationship, the closing of a door or the shattering of a dream,
grief is ultimately the process of coming to terms with loss,
and with loss there is always pain. There's lots written about
grief, the process and the various stages we go through which
is all really helpful. The danger with this, however, is we can
succumb to the notion that we are robots who mechanically
pass through each stage of the grief cycle in a linear way, but
we are 'wonderfully and fearfully made' (Psalm 139:14) and we
are not robots but human beings. This means at times we don't
journey through each stage smoothly or evenly; sometimes we
get stuck, sometimes we circle back, sometimes we find we are
living in each stage at the same time even on the same day.

Recently I heard a helpful description of what grief can be like
and it was this: imagine grief is like being followed by a dog
every day of your life. Some days that dog is a small chihuahua
and can be easily ignored or shooed away. Other days that dog
is a huge German shepherd and everything stops to orientate
around that dog on that day. To add to this thought, I came to
realise several years ago that God has two 'dogs' that follow us
every day of our lives described in the great psalm of comfort,
Psalm 23: 'Surely goodness and mercy shall follow me all the
days of my life' (Psalm 23:6, NKJV).

In this incredible psalm about us being the sheep and God our
shepherd, could it be that God's two sheepdogs are goodness
and mercy who follow us every day of our lives, even the days
that are marked by pain and grief?

In the embracing of grief and the journey of dealing with our
pain, we can get stuck, and in those moments there is the
danger that we can transfer that pain rather than allowing

God to transform it. 'Hurt people can hurt people' so be careful not to transfer your pain into something that hurts or harms yourself or others. Let God transform your pain, or you will transfer your pain in some other way. The greater story of God is where God meets us in our pain; after all, he is the God in the middle of the story with all of its unresolved tension, longing and questions, and he stands with us right in the middle of our pain.

> If your heart is broken, you'll find GOD right there; if you're kicked in the gut, he›ll help you catch your breath.
>
> (Psalm 34:18, *The Message*)

When you're in pain, don't let that pain alone define you

This is a tough one to speak about, but there are times when the pain we experience becomes synonymous with our identity. It relates to a previous chapter when the man at the pool at Bethesda was asked, 'Do you want to get well?' (John 5:6). Sometimes, as painful as it might be to admit, we actually don't want the pain to go, sometimes we even need that pain, or we think we do. In the *Star Trek* film, *The Final Frontier*,[56] there's a classic scene where Captain Kirk angrily confront Bones, the doctor, insisting pain can't be taken away with some kind of magic wand. Then he ends his rant with the words, 'I don't want my pain taken away ... I need my pain.' Sobering words.

Jesus invites us to surrender our pain to him; after all, our identity is not to be found in our pain but in who he says we are even with our pain. Having said this, there are some pains in our lives that shape us into who we are and who we are becoming. For some of us it's living with lifelong conditions;

maybe we are caring for others and all kinds of other life-defining situations. Even then it's not the pain alone that should define us, but the hand of our Creator on our life – as we saw earlier in Isaiah, the potter shaping the clay even through and in the pain. Then remember there's still something else our redeemer would want us to look for and it's this ...

When you're in pain, look for the gold

Recently my wife came back from visiting a woman in our church who has been housebound for many months due to a chronic long-term illness. She is young, vibrant, intelligent with two teenage children and yet she can hardly ever leave the house. She has become an integral part of our online church community and as my wife spent time with her, she came away more encouraged and humbled by this lady and her startling faith. In her pain she spoke of learning to invest her suffering, of learning to partner with God in redeeming the pain for her good and for others; she is finding the gold in her pain. This is the redemption Isaiah was speaking about. It's often through our pain that we discover new things about ourselves and about God. It's often through our pain that we develop empathy and compassion for others and are then able to help them in their pain journeys. Instead of praying so often 'Lord, *when* can I get out of this?' maybe we should adjust the prayer to, 'Lord, *what* can I get out of this?' Maybe the circumstances we ask God to change are the very thing God is using to change us?

When it finally felt like we were all emerging from the COVID crisis, I often found myself saying, 'The only thing worse than a crisis is a wasted crisis.' Maybe it's also true of our pain; let's not waste that pain but ask God to help us redeem that pain, and mine that pain for some gold for our lives and maybe for others' lives too. Paul expresses this idea beautifully in

2 Corinthians when he exhorts us to see our pain and grief through a redemptive lens:

> Praise be to the God and Father of our Lord Jesus Christ, the Father of compassion and the God of all comfort, who comforts us in all our troubles, so that we can comfort those in any trouble with the comfort we ourselves receive from God.
> (2 Corinthians 1:3-4)

A few words on how we can help others who find themselves in the middle of pain, grief or loss.

Firstly, don't avoid them

This is so often the inclination because we don't know what to say and we don't want to say anything that could make people feel worse. The reality is, there's not much we could say that could make people feel any worse, but the worse thing is to be ignored. In truth, just showing up and sitting with someone and not saying anything is help enough. I heard the late Tony Campolo tell a story of when he went to a funeral of a friend only to discover he was at the wrong funeral. The only mourner was the widow and so Tony stayed with her through the whole service, and at the end he confessed he didn't know her husband. 'I know,' she said gently squeezing his arm, 'but you will never know what being here has meant to me.'[57]

Secondly, don't try to outdo them with your pain

I'm constantly staggered at how often people ask a question of someone in pain and then proceed to tell them of their pain stories, rather than listening to the person they first asked! 'That's like my life ... that's nothing compared to what has happened to me ...' Those kinds of responses don't bring comfort, they just create further pain.

Thirdly, don't try to ease your awkwardness with easy, cheap, or trite words

Sometimes all people need is to know we are there, we care and we are willing to sit in that place of awkwardness or silence long enough to make a connection. We don't have all the answers and even if we did, they wouldn't be enough anyway. You see, there's something else we need to remember in the living room of life and it's this: *When you're in pain remember something better is coming.*

Your story is not over and as we will see in Part Three, God is not only redeeming and recreating but he is perfecting; one day your pain will be totally transformed and you will see Jesus face to face, and the promise for that day is that there will be no more ... pain.

> Pain isn't the worst thing. Being hated isn't the worst thing. Being separated from the one you love isn't the worst thing. Death isn't the worst thing. The worst thing is failing to deal with reality and becoming disconnected from what is actual ... what I do with my grief affects the way you handle your grief, together we form a community that deals with death and other loss in context of God's sovereignty and expressed finally in resurrection.
>
> (Eugene Peterson)[58]

God is greater than our pain.

- Talk to Jesus about the pain you are currently carrying.

- What's one step you could take to help invest your pain?

A prayer for when pain feels unbearable

Lord, at times I sense I'm alone with my pain.
At times I'm not even sure you are aware of my pain.
Yet when I consider Jesus, I know none of this is true.
I know you not only see my pain, you feel my pain and you can transform my pain.
Help me to surrender that pain to you, help me to find purpose in the pain.
For you are greater than my pain.

Amen

CHAPTER NINE

Greater Than Our Doubts

Trust in the LORD for ever,
for the LORD GOD is an everlasting rock.

(Isaiah 26:4, ESV)

Faith and doubt are both needed, not as antagonists,
but working side by side to take us around the
unknown curve.

(Lillian Smith)[59]

It was the Year 9 inter-house rugby final and I was safe – at least I thought I was. You see, I hated rugby with a passion, it was way too violent and way too intense for me, so I sat on the hillside watching the brutes slug it out. All was well until one guy in my house got injured and the PE teacher bellowed, 'Evans, you're on, get changed!' Reluctantly, I got changed and dragged myself to the pitch to be met by my nemesis. This guy was huge and he resembled an orc from *Lord of the Rings* rather than a fourteen-year-old boy. For some reason he hated me, and so when he saw me enter the 'arena' he screamed, 'Evans, when you get the ball, I'm going to smash you!' Instantly, as if I'd had divine revelation from heaven, I knew my strategy for the game, 'Don't go anywhere near the ball.' The thing is it worked . . . until it didn't. The scores were level and for some inexplicable reason someone threw me the ball and I caught it. To this day I have no idea why. At that moment I had options: drop the ball clumsily, throw the ball away hastily, hide the ball up my top and pretend it wasn't there, or run with it. I chose to run and boy, did I run. Nathan was screaming behind me, fire bellowing from his flaring nostrils, talons scraping down my back, but I ran. I ran so fast that I crossed the touch line and kept on running, until the PE teacher yelled, 'Evans, touch the ball down!' so I did and we won the game. I'd love to tell you that the story ended with me being lifted on shoulders and paraded around the pitch as a conquering hero, but it didn't. I did, however, learn a lesson that day and it's this: *When the ball comes to you, you have a choice about what you will do.*

In this epic adventure God invites us into of seeing the world redeemed and re-created, there are many moments when the ball will come to you. At that moment you have a choice of what you will do. One of the 'balls' that comes to all of us from time to time is doubt. It can come when we least expect it, and when it comes we have a choice: we can drop it, we can try to hide it pretending it isn't there, or we can run with it. When we choose to run with it, here's the thing: then we get the chance to encounter the God who is *greater* than our doubts. Not only that, but we will come to discover that doubt is not the enemy we thought it was; in fact, doubt can be a doorway into greater faith.

When it comes to faith, everybody doubts, even atheists doubt!

C.S. Lewis said, 'Now that I am a Christian I do have moods in which the whole thing looks very improbable: but when I was an atheist I had moods in which Christianity looked terribly probable.'[60]

If you are not a Christian, you can doubt the existence of God.

If you are a Christian, you can doubt the goodness of God.

You might say, 'I can't believe in God because I have doubts.'

You might say, 'I can't trust God because I have doubts.'

We don't live life this way as life is full of doubts; take relationships, for example. If you remove doubt or uncertainty, you have no need for faith or trust, then what do you have? In the film *The Stepford Wives*, set in a dystopian America, the wives were all robots. True there was no uncertainty, no doubt, I mean husbands knew what they would get every day. The wife would be dressed immaculately, the house cleaned top to bottom, the meal prepared when they got in, she was there for his every wish but she was not real, she was a robot. Relationships were never meant to be robotic or, indeed, that predictable. An element of doubt in any relationship is a dose of reality, and with it an entrance into the mystery and adventure of what it means to be human and to connect with others. This is also true of our relationship with God; it was never meant to be robotic, so there will always be the possibility of some measure of doubt.

Without doubt, you wouldn't need faith

Doubt is not the opposite of faith; unbelief is the opposite of faith, and that's a different 'ball' entirely. There once was a man who made doubting world-famous; in fact, doubt became an appendage to his name and he is known as 'doubting Thomas'. Thomas gets a bad press from many, including the Church, but I love Thomas. I love his passion, his curiosity, his authenticity and as you study his life and the way he ran with his ball of doubt, there are so many lessons for us and our story. We read in John's account of the post-resurrection appearances of Jesus, and the moment the ball of doubt came to Thomas:

> Now Thomas (also known as Didymus), one of the Twelve, was not with the disciples when Jesus came. So the other disciples told him, 'We have seen the Lord!' But he said to them, 'Unless I see the nail marks in his hands and put my finger where the nails were, and put my hand into his side, I will not believe.'
>
> (John 20:24-25)

Thomas wants to believe but he has doubts, why? He wasn't there when everyone else saw the resurrected Jesus, he didn't see what the others saw, and you have to feel for him. How many of us have had moments when everyone else was talking about the game they watched, the mountain they climbed, the show they enjoyed, the festival they went to and we missed it? We are so 'happy' for them, but deep down also a little unsure as to whether it was quite as amazing as they claimed. I mean, we weren't there so how do we know, right?

Thomas was also called 'Didymus', which means twin or two, and doubt is actually to be in two minds:

> Belief is to be in one mind accepting
> Unbelief is to be in one mind rejecting
> Doubt is to be in two minds

You can be Christian, a follower of Jesus, and still have some doubts. What's more, you can have doubts and still play a part in the adventure of God's story, as long as you choose to run with the ball. To doubt means we are not sure. It's not the same as unbelief, which is where we are sure and have reached a conclusion and invariably it means we've arrived at a place where we turn our backs on God. But doubt is to stay open because deep down we want to believe, we are just not sure.

Another character who had doubts was John the Baptist. If there was anyone who was in the game and running with the ball it was him, right? He was full of woes just like Isaiah, calling people to repentance, and people were responding in their hundreds and thousands. He was preparing the way of the Lord. Surely, he wouldn't have any doubts? Then he is put in prison later, to be paraded as a plaything for malevolent leaders, and in Matthew's Gospel we read these sobering words ...

> After Jesus had finished instructing his twelve disciples, he went on from there to teach and preach in the towns of Galilee. When John, who was in prison, heard about the deeds of the Messiah, he sent his disciples to ask him, 'Are you the one who is to come, or should we expect someone else?'
>
> (Matthew 11:1-3)

I find these words both penetrating and painful. John articulates what has gone through all of our minds at some point or another: 'Are you the one ... did I get it wrong trusting in you, Lord? Did I back the wrong horse? How can this story be true if this is where I've ended up?'

Let's make a few things really clear ...

Doubt is not a virus that will destroy you, if you work with it

Immunisation is a dose of the illness in order to strengthen antibodies and actually make you stronger. Doubt can be like that; it can make you stronger if you deal with it well. The author Madelaine L'Engle puts it this way: 'Those who believe they believe in God but without passion in the heart, without anguish of mind, without uncertainty, without doubt, and even at times without despair, believe only in the idea of God, and not in God himself.'[61]

Mother Teresa famously wrote letters in her diaries discovered after her death. Within these letters she reveals that while she did know times of intimacy with Jesus, there were many years where she felt her prayers were greeted by silence, and she confessed to doubts even to the existence of God.[62]

So, if this is ever your experience, you are in good company but keep running with the 'ball'. Having said that, there is another side to doubt, and it's this:

Doubt can be dangerous if left untreated

If you don't catch the ball and run with it, if you drop it, discard it, try to hide it or pretend it doesn't exist, something will happen within you. It won't happen immediately and it's likely to happen in stages;

Stage 1: the **Sceptic** – someone who suspends judgement: 'I'm just not sure it's true.'

This was Thomas; he wasn't sure, but he wanted it to be true. If you stay here too long you get trapped, you miss out on so much, but even worse than that, you can find yourself moving to the next stage . . .

Stage 2: the **Cynic** – someone not looking for answers but offering conclusions, and they are nearly always negative: 'It can't be true.'

Give a sceptic a hug and they will doubt you really mean it, give a cynic a hug and they will check their wallet! Cynics are often wounded idealists; the whole world is wrong, faith and trust are foreign concepts. Stay here too long and you can end up in the final stage . . .

Stage 3: the **Rebel** – someone who doesn't want to believe, who doesn't want the story of Jesus to be true; it doesn't matter what the evidence is, they wouldn't accept it: 'It mustn't be true.'

So, what can we say to the Thomases and Johns of this world? God will prove he is greater than our doubts ... how?

What John needed God gave him; he only needed to hear from Jesus again:

> Jesus replied, 'Go back and report to John what you hear and see: the blind receive sight, the lame walk, those who have leprosy are cleansed, the deaf hear, the dead are raised, and the good news is proclaimed to the poor.
>
> (Matthew 11:4-5)

I can picture John in his cell with a wry smile on his face: 'Now I get it, the story is true, God is redeeming the world to himself in and through Jesus. What's happening to me is painful and uncomfortable, but it's OK because God is greater than my doubts.'

What Thomas needed God gave him. He only needed to see Jesus for himself:

> A week later his disciples were in the house again, and Thomas was with them. Though the doors were locked, Jesus came and stood among them and said, 'Peace be with you!' Then he said to Thomas, 'Put your finger here; see my hands. Reach out your hand and put it into my side. Stop doubting and believe.' Thomas said to him, 'My Lord and my God!' Then Jesus told him, 'Because you have seen me, you have believed; blessed are those who have not seen and yet have believed.'
>
> (John 20:26-29)

I love Thomas for this so much. A week later he hasn't gone anywhere, he is still running with the ball, he is still hanging around the community of faith and then Jesus shows up and proves he is *greater* than Thomas' doubts. So many of us, when we have doubts, we back away from church and community, and that is usually the wrong thing to do because Jesus loves to show up where his people gather, as he did for Thomas.

A final word on Thomas. Church history and tradition suggest Thomas took the gospel of Jesus to India, and having been to Southern India many times, I've seen the legacy as churches are named after this man known in that part of the world not so much for his doubt but for his faith. Tradition suggests Thomas was martyred for his faith and maybe even by a spear thrust into his side. If that were true, how ironic and fitting would that be, given the marks Jesus showed him in his hands, feet and side. You see when you run with the 'ball' of doubt it can actually strengthen your faith, it can be a doorway into greater faith because ... *God is greater than our doubts.*

- What's the ball of doubt you are carrying right now?
- What do you need to hear from God?
- How do you need to encounter God?

A prayer for when you catch the ball of doubt

Lord, here I am holding this ball of doubt (again).
I choose to run with the doubt, not drop it, hide it or pretend it doesn't exist.
I choose to run towards you, not away from you.
Help this doubt; be a doorway that leads me to greater faith.
For you are greater than my doubts.

Amen

The
Playground

For all the resources and links mentioned,
scan the code to visit
www.springharvest.org/resources/no-greater-story

CHAPTER TEN

The Redeemer in the Playground

We've been in the classroom looking at the *what*, we've been in the living room looking at the *so what*, now we turn to the *now what* and we head to the playground where everyone gets to play their part in the greater story.

My life

Here's an activity you can do . . .

Take a large piece of paper, turn it landscape, and in the middle draw a line that will act as a timeline.

Above the line, write the key milestone events from your life that have been positive, and under the line the ones that have been difficult or challenging.

Somewhere along that timeline, draw a cross to represent when you became a Christian, or when you started following Jesus seriously.

As you work on this timeline, you might want to consider plotting not just events but other things such as significant people, seasons of emotional difficulty, moments of great joy that you carry all your life and others that come to mind.

Once you've spent some time creating your story timeline, reflect with these questions:

- What strikes me from my timeline?
- What surprises me?
- What are the three biggest events that have shaped me into who I am today?
- Where do I see God at work as redeemer in my life and story?

Timelines like these help us see our story from a different vantage point. They help us make connections, join dots and see patterns. They help us grieve, they also help us celebrate, they help us see and remember what we may have forgotten, they also remind us our story is not over and that there is an author and it's not us. God has been at work in our story and he will continue to be at work as we follow him.

As you reflect on your timeline and what God has done so far in your story, one of the privileges we get as a follower of Jesus is the ability to share our story, our journey of faith. It's also one of the things we find the most difficult to do. I remember years ago hearing someone suggest that the longer we go on as a follower of Jesus, the less effective we are at sharing our faith. The reason for this is that over time we know less people who don't have faith and we lose our confidence to share our faith. Rediscovering your part in God's epic adventure story should include sharing your story with others. Multiple research projects over years suggest most people become Christians as children, or through another Christian sharing their faith with them. So, how do we do it?

Here are a few simple tips to get started:

Think of your story in three simple stages, BC, the cross, AD.
BC is what life was like before you knew Jesus, the cross is how
you came to faith and AD is what life is like now after you've
come to Christ.

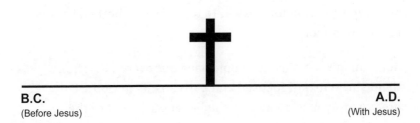

B.C.   **A.D.**
(Before Jesus)   (With Jesus)

As you craft your story, try to keep it short, a few minutes.

As you craft your story, keep it jargon free, lose the words that
need a lot of explanation.

As you craft your story, resist the urge to compare to others
who seem to have a more dramatic story. Your story is real,
your story is valid and your story is what God will use to
impact others.

A few other things to remember: we don't only share our
stories with words, we also share it with actions. We must be
sensitive; the goal isn't to 'win' or to 'get our story across',
the goal is to build a bridge that Jesus by his Spirit can walk
across. We must be willing to play the long game, to invest in
relationship, to invite to events and opportunities and, when
it's right, to share our own story.

To help you explore this further, I want to recommend a free
resource developed by a friend of mine, Mark Greenwood, and

it's called Boot Camp Lite. Mark is the national evangelist for the Elim Pentecostal Church and a good friend who has helped our church stay outward focused to reach many people who didn't know Jesus.[63]

There are also details of a great resource from Marie-Louise Aitken from Alpha UK called 'Keep it Simple'[64] which is a book and video series helping us all to learn how to better share our redemption story.

Something I know many people have discovered that helps them stay outward focused and participants in God's greater story is to sponsor a child in another part of the world. Organisations such as Compassion do an amazing job helping lift children out of poverty. Here's the thing: if you impact a child, you impact a family, and if you impact enough families, you impact a community, and if you impact enough communities, you can change a nation. As a church, we partner with Compassion and support more than 200 children worldwide. My wife and I had the privilege in 2024 to visit the community project we support in Tanzania and visit the children we support personally – life-changing is an understatement![65]

For more information on how you could get involved, visit the information via the QR code.

My home

Whoever you share your home with, try out some of these creative activities, and if there are children in the your home, get them together and dive into these amazing ideas from Care for the Family called the Kitchen Table Project. And remember, faith grows as you go![66]

As you go . . . to eat

Share high and low points from the day as you eat. Thank God for the highs and pray for the lows together.

As a family, think of ways to help those who don't have enough food.

As you go . . . out

When you go swimming think of a Bible story that involves water, like Jonah and the big fish or Peter walking on the water. What do these stories teach us about God as our Creator and Saviour?

At sunrise or sunset, talk about God as an artist and praise him for all the colours.

As you go . . . around the house

Build a den and talk about how God is our safe place and fortress, he is greater than anything we might fear.

Put worship music on and ask your kids to build or make something – Lego, paints or Play-Doh – whatever your child wants to use.

As you go . . . to bed

Set aside some time to talk about the questions children often have at bedtime instead of waiting until the morning.

Read a psalm or blessing like Numbers 6:24-26 over your children.

As you go . . . to church

Talk about what you learned in the sermon so your kids know you've been learning too!

Find a family prayer buddy and pick a time each week to pray for each other.

My church

Your church has a story; maybe it's not always been the story you've wanted, but it's part of the story of God.

Invite a few others from your fellowship to draw out a story timeline of your church. Plot some of the key events and milestones of your church's story, similar to what you did above.

- What impacts you from this story timeline?
- What are you thankful to God for?
- What would be your one prayer for your church's future?

Jesus was the first person to mention the word 'church' in the New Testament in Matthew 16:18 when he declared, 'I will build my church'. He went on to say that his Church would be unstoppable, because the Church is conceived in the heart, mind and will of God, birthed and brought to life by a single event, the resurrection of Jesus, and sustained by the Spirit of God. Maybe you don't see your church this way every time you roll up on a Sunday, but what you are a part of is something way bigger, majestic, beautiful and powerful than you could ever imagine. The Church is the instrument God is using to bring his kingdom to earth, to redeem the earth, to ultimately perfect his will in all creation. The problem is, we've lost sight of what the Church really is. When Jesus used the word 'church' for the first time, he actually used the Greek word *ekklesia*. This word had common meaning and understanding in the ancient world; it referred to an assembly of people gathered for purpose. We say it in our church like this: we are meant to be an outward-facing, multicultural, multi-generational, multiplying movement. Over the passage of time, the word 'church' ended up translated to mean a building you go to rather than a movement you belong to.

For our churches to play their part in the greater story of God, we must rediscover who we were always meant to be, and that means fighting the bias every church possesses. Just like the bias in a bowling ball, every church has three biases: we turn inward, we grow old and we disconnect from our culture. The story of God requires a church that fights those biases and remains an outward-focused, multiplying movement.

How do we do that, and how does your church play its part?

For many years, our church has been trying to fight these biases and then in 2018, along with other like-minded churches, we started an organisation called the Further Faster Network, with the sole aim of encouraging, inspiring and equipping churches in the UK and Ireland to create outward-facing churches that were reaching unchurched people with the good news of the story of God.[67] One of the key foundational principles we gather around is the idea that as churches we should be *for* our community. So often the Church is known for what it is against rather than what it is *for*. The irony is, God loved the world so much that he gave Jesus, and Jesus was known as the 'friend of . . . sinners' (Matthew 11:19). In fact, people who were nothing like Jesus liked Jesus and wanted to be around him! Does the community around your church know you're there, are they glad you're there, and are they better off because you are there? We say it this way: 'We don't want to be the best church *in* our community but the best church *for* our community.'

Some years ago, we were approaching a church anniversary and one of our team found a social media post that commented on our town, and it suggested our town was the place dreams go to die! We were shocked! Our town may not be the most glamorous (it really isn't!) but it's our town, and we are called to be there and to be *for* it. So, we took a hold of that phrase and at a large community event encouraged literally hundreds of people to write their dream for our town, whether they had faith or not, and we released those dreams into the air. We believe that was a prophetic and pivotal moment for our church and our town as we have seen incredible growth and community impact since that day.

Why don't you gather some people in your church and use these questions to generate discussion and prayer for your church and for your community?

- What's the story of our community around our church?
- What are the challenges our community faces?
- What are the hopes and aspirations of people in our community?
- How does our community see our church?
- How do we know how they see us?
- In what ways can we as a church be more *for* our community?
- What would it take for our church to become more outward-focused?

To help you with this, the network we are a part of has a free assessment tool you might want to encourage your leadership to take. It will give them a comprehensive print out around the principles of being an outward-facing church that grows by reaching unchurched people. You can access that survey via our website which you can find using the QR code.

Top ten tips for being a more outward-facing church:

1. Make sure your mission and vision reflect the call to be outward-facing.

2. Invite an unchurched person to come and sit with you in church *(this will impact how you see church)*.

3. Celebrate stories that remind people why we do what we do.

4. Welcome the mess *(if you want a nice, tidy, neat church, don't be outward-facing!)*.

5. Assume they're in the room *(by this I mean watch your language, jargon, insider jokes)*.

6. Build a culture of love and generosity.

7. Find ways you can serve your wider community with no strings attached.

8. Think steps not programmes *(evaluate all you do with this question: 'How does this help people take a step either towards Jesus or growing in Jesus?)*

9. Visit other churches that are doing it well and learn from them.

10. Embrace change *(the last words of a dying church: 'We have never done it that way before')*.

One more thought: the power of the early Church wasn't just the presence of the Spirit of Jesus, it was the way they loved one another; it was the power of community, of family. Family is such a loaded word, but deep in the heart of God's story is the idea that we as churches would model family that includes all people, whatever age or stage of life they happen to be. One of the most effective ways we can do that is through fostering and adoption, and Church lives out the greater story of God when we provide homes for those who don't have one. The Church I have the privilege of leading is so much richer for the many adopted and fostered children and young people we have, as well as many with additional needs. One of the organisations that provides help, advice, encouragement and support is Home For Good.[68] Check out their incredible work and learn what it could mean for your church to become that safe place for children to find healing, hope and home. This is all part of God's greater story of redemption, and we can all play our part in that adventure.

PART THREE
Perfecter

**Completer, Finisher,
Enabler . . .**

Devil trying to take on Michael
Cast out of heaven
He was taking the Michael
Like the Almighty was in retirement
But the King returns
Speaks his reprisal
As a book is opened
Lamb reads a recital
About a curse that's broken
A people chosen
In the blood
He is baptising
Where I saw graveclothes
Now I see saints arising
Clothed in a garment
Made of diamonds
Worn in the garden where it all begun
Tell me that's not poetic timing
Where is this heading?
An intimate picture of an ending
The invitation of Scripture to a wedding
Make way for the groom
The bride awaits
He steps out the throne room
The robe stained with crimson
He lifts her veil
To reveal his kingdom
Mouth a sword
Moving in a new rhythm
Unbelief receding
Peace increasing
Not a wrinkle in time

The page of history is creasing
At the voice of a Father
Who never stopped speaking
After the fast
Came the feasting
A celebration
The information says the Son of Man
Is liable to libations
But we're not under the influence
We speak under inspiration
Because the wait is over
God descended
And he bought his mates over
Tears are wiped
But this ain't a makeover
Kingdom of heaven established
This is the takeover

The
Classroom

See, I will create
new heavens and a new earth.
The former things will not be remembered,
nor will they come to mind.
But be glad and rejoice for ever
in what I will create,
for I will create Jerusalem to be a delight
and its people a joy.
I will rejoice over Jerusalem
and take delight in my people;
the sound of weeping and of crying
will be heard in it no more.

(Isaiah 65:17-19)

That is what the Scriptures mean when they
say, 'No eye has seen, no ear has heard,
and no mind has imagined what God has
prepared for those who love him.'

(1 Corinthians 2:9, NLT. See also Isaiah 64:4, 65:17.
The apostle Paul and Isaiah)

CHAPTER ELEVEN

God at the End

We are all tempted at times to compare and contrast our story with others. At times our own story feels dull and mundane compared to what we perceive others' stories to be. Ours can feel like a Sunday evening period drama compared to others' Hollywood blockbusters, yet all of our stories have certain things in common.

Firstly, everybody has a story and everybody's story really matters to God. Secondly, nobody gets the story they wanted ... not really. We all live in a second choice, or, at times, even a no-choice world, and with it comes the realisation that our story is not the story we dreamed or envisaged it would be. Thirdly, when our story becomes part of God's greater story, everything changes. Now the narrative is broader, now the horizon is further, now the meaning is deeper. Our story can find redemption, meaning and purpose when it becomes part of God's greater story.

If there's one thing we are all looking for in life it's value. We replace that at times with what we think adds value, like success, significance, wealth, possession, relationships, or security, yet none of these add the value we long for. In fact, it's the story that adds value to anything. Let me explain. If I were to offer you a glass as a gift, you wouldn't be impressed. But if I were to tell you it's the glass Winston Churchill drank from in the bunkers underneath Whitehall where he planned the D-Day landing during the Second World War, all of a sudden the value of that glass changes! It's the story that adds the value. Your story adds value because God created you and has a plan for you, and he is working that plan out in your story and as part of his greater story.

What Isaiah sees for his nation, and prophetically for all that are to follow, is the greater story of God that has its beginning in God as the Creator, the Author, the Originator, the Playwright, if you like. Then he sees the middle of the story, how God incarnated himself, which in essence meant he wrote himself into his own story in the form of Jesus, who Isaiah described as the suffering servant. In Part Three of this epic adventure, we turn our attention to the end of the story, because every good story has a beginning, a middle and an ... end.

It was Aristotle who famously said that in storytelling the ending must be both 'unexpected and inevitable'.[69] His thought was that a great story has a surprising ending, yet one that also seems satisfying and predictable, as if that was the way it was meant to be. We've all sat through movies or Box Sets on TV gripped by the story and anticipating the ending, only to be left deflated and unsatisfied when the ending caught us by surprise, or left us asking more questions than finding answers.

The other thing about story is this: central to an engaging story will always be the theme of desire. The central character in any great story has a desire, and the strength of that desire runs through the story giving that story weight, meaning and intrigue. *The stronger the desire, the greater the story.*

Let's take a few minutes to think not about you, me or any of our stories, but the central character in God's story . . . God himself. What's God's desire in his story?

Dallas Willard beautifully expressed it this way: 'The aim of God in history is the creation of an all-inclusive community of loving persons, with Himself included in that community as its prime sustainer and most glorious inhabitant.'[70]

That's where this story is heading, an eternal community or, as Isaiah often likened it, a new heaven and a new earth. The late Tim Keller put it this way: 'Our Christian hope is that we are going to live with Christ in a new earth, where there is not only no more death, but where life is what it was always meant to be.'[71]

Chapter 56 onwards sees Isaiah embark on the final part of his prophetic foray into the greater story of God. In terms of the context of his day, historically we are now in a time where the first returners are coming back to Jerusalem from exile in Babylon. In broad terms, it's the era of Ezra and Nehemiah, it's the era of the rebuilding of the walls and the restoration of the city gates. It's the time where God was intent on seeing his people displaying his character and nature to his world. It was the time where what had been broken and dislocated was to become whole and connected once again.

God is on a mission to make all things new

During this season of history, Israel finds herself in a time of high expectation and high anxiety. It's a season marked by geo-political unrest and instability. The economy is unstable, as nations around the region posture and jostle for power and supremacy. It is a difficult task to establish a secure and viable community who will express and live out the greater story of God. In reality, they are living in a season that could be described as a 'grey zone' we spoke about in the introduction, an era 'between the times'. The exile has begun but is not complete; they are living in an in-between space, between 'now' and 'not yet'.

The apostle Paul describes this type of experience in Romans 8:22 when he says, 'We know that the whole creation has been groaning as in the pains of childbirth right up to the present time.'

This experience of living 'between the times' is not only a common one, it's a painful one. It's the time we find ourselves waiting for the new world that we sense and hope is around the corner, yet we don't fully know how long it will be till we reach that corner or how long that corner might actually be! In a real sense, since the moment the suffering servant (Jesus) experienced his death and resurrection, we are now in this period of waiting for what's to come; we are living between the times, between the trees mentioned in the Garden of Eden (Genesis 2:9) and the tree mentioned in John's revelation of the new heaven and new earth (Revelation 22:2); we are living in what the Bible calls, 'the last days' (2 Timothy 3:1).

The last days is such a popular theme for Christians to get worked up about; in fact, I love what I once heard a preacher say when he spoke about what was most on the minds of Christian young people. He said if you want to pique the interest of Christian teenagers, speak on one of three themes:

1. Sex

2. The end times

3. Will there be sex in the end times!

I want to suggest it's not just Christian teenagers who are fascinated by the end times (notice I didn't say sex there!). Isaiah paints a picture for us of what this period of waiting could look like that resonates deeply as we look around and consider our world in these days and in this cultural moment. He talks of a shaking that appears, especially due to the quality of the spiritual leadership of the day. In Chapter 56 to 57 he pulls no punches describing the leaders during this season:

> Israel's watchmen are blind,
> they all lack knowledge;
> they are all mute dogs,
> they cannot bark;
> they lie around and dream,
> they love to sleep.
> They are dogs with mighty appetites;
> they never have enough.
> They are shepherds who lack understanding;
> they all turn to their own way,
> they seek their own gain.
>
> (Isaiah 56:10-11)

The terms 'watchmen' and 'shepherds' are important biblical words describing the kind of spiritual leadership we should aspire to. The idea of a 'watchman' is that this person is observant, looking out for the people under their care, anticipating where harm or danger could come and wanting the best for the people they are leading. The 'shepherd' metaphor is intensely powerful and important in the Bible and speaks to what leadership should be about, not just in Bible times but also in our times. Shepherds are there for the sheep, not the other way round. If you are a leader of any description, let me remind you, the people are not there for you but you are there for them. I remember being at a local authority meeting years ago where the leader of the council declared he had discovered a new leadership concept called 'servant leadership'. I smiled to myself. 'It's not new,' I thought, 'and in fact it's the only kind there should be in the truest meaning of what leadership was designed to be.' In recent times the Christian Church has been rocked by scandal after scandal, investigation after investigation over abuses of power, toxic cultures and worse. It's easy when we find ourselves in seasons like this to feel that darkness is winning, but actually it's just evidence that God is moving. Sometimes God's timing is an expression of God's kindness and I sense the Lord is cleaning up his Church as he requires and desires; a Church that's holy and set apart for his purposes in his story. It's easy for these scandals and revelations to leave us all with a sense of despondency and disappointment. Here's the truth about disappointment...

Disappointments don't line up, they stack up

The weight of disappointment on top of disappointment can bear down heavily on our souls, but God is writing a greater story and he is not only in the beginning and the middle, he will also be at the end. After all, he has a vested interest in how this story plays out. He is not only the Author, but as the writer of Hebrews in chapter 12:2 says, he is also the Perfecter. Just a cursory glance at different translations gives us the range of meaning that these evocative words have. Here are just a few:

> The 'pioneer and perfecter' (NIVUK), the 'author and finisher' (NKJV), the 'champion who initiates and perfects' (NLT), the 'founder and perfecter' (ESV).

Isaiah saw the future and encourages the people to stay in the story because God was staying in the story, his story, working out all things according to his timing and will:

I am GOD, the only God you've had or ever will have –
incomparable, irreplaceable –
From the very beginning
 telling you what the ending will be,
All along letting you in
 on what is going to happen,
Assuring you, 'I'm in this for the long haul,
 I'll do exactly what I set out to do . . .'

(Isaiah 46:9-10, *The Message*)

In the words of a classic TV quiz show, God might say, 'I've started so I'll finish!'[72]

Isaiah then highlights some other key things that will happen in this part of God's story.

His people will shine

Arise, shine, for your light has come,
 and the glory of the LORD rises upon you.
See, darkness covers the earth
 and thick darkness is over the peoples,
but the LORD rises upon you
 and his glory appears over you.
Nations will come to your light,
 and kings to the brightness of your dawn.

(Isaiah 60:1-3)

This chapter is really interesting in how it is constructed from a literary standpoint. There are ten stanzas and all except one have eight lines, five stanzas on each side of what Alec Motyer calls the 'dark pivot' which he refers to as verse 12:[73] 'For the nation or kingdom that will not serve you will perish; it will be utterly ruined' (Isaiah 60:12).

This references the Abrahamic idea that those who bless God will themselves become a blessing for the world. Even though Isaiah is imagining the restoration of Zion (Jerusalem), this is way beyond a mere city, this is the culmination of God's greater story, this is pointing towards the new heaven and the new earth. Isaiah is the only prophet to use light in any notable way. As he does, it's a reference back to Genesis 1 where God said, 'Let there be light' (Genesis 1:3) and it also points towards John 1 where Jesus is referenced as 'the light of all mankind' (John 1:4).

The interesting fact to note in these verses is that Isaiah sees a day when the light will be generated purely from God himself, even though he would have witnessed the sun coming up over Jerusalem many times. Nations that willingly serve and come to the Lord will be blessed and those that won't will suffer difficulty. Isaiah paints a picture of the new order that is to come; the comfort promised in Isaiah 40 is realised here, the restoration promised earlier is realised here, the fear and threat of the old order has gone. There's a sense of pervading peace and security that the people have never known before and was only found in the Garden of Eden right at the beginning of the story. Not only will his people shine...

His kingdom will be established

This prophetic picture of the future describes a time when all people will come to the knowledge of the glory of God. It's very easy in our Western, post-, some people say pre-, Christian context to think of the Church as declining and the glory of the Lord dissipating, but that is not the reality when you consider what is happening around the world. According to the Gordon-Conwell Theological Seminar's 2024 report, Christianity is growing around the world faster than the rate of population!

In fact, the Christian population is predicted to top 3 billion before 2050.[74] The fastest growing areas for Christianity are the Global South; by 2050, the African Christian population is predicted to swell to 1.28 billion. In my own experience, I have witnessed some of the rapid growth in Christianity around the world. In South Korea at the turn of the twentieth century there were hardly any Christians, but by the 1980s almost a third of the population professed to be Christians. I remember visiting the then largest church in the world, Yoido Full Gospel Church, Seoul, and being blown away by the size of the building. As I got out of the taxi, I saw a huge skyscraper, but soon came to realise that what I was actually looking at was not the main auditorium of the church but the building for the children's work! The main auditorium was even bigger and I couldn't yet see it. The reason I want to remind us all of these facts and trends is not to advocate a 'big is beautiful or better' idea, but merely to remind us all that Jesus is still building his Church, and when it seems to die in one part of the world, it will come to life in another. When it declines in one place, it is growing in another; you can't stop it, you can't ultimately keep it down or eliminate it, because it doesn't originate in the mind of man but in the heart and will of God. It's his Church, it's his body, it's his bride and it's his story.

Isaiah then reminds the people of two key ideas in Jewish thought, namely the day of vengeance and the 'year of the Lord's favour':

> The Spirit of the Sovereign Lord is on me,
> because the Lord has anointed me
> to proclaim good news to the poor.
> He has sent me to bind up the broken-hearted,
> to proclaim freedom for the captives
> and release from darkness for the prisoners,

to proclaim the year of the LORD's favour
and the day of vengeance of our God,
to comfort all who mourn . . .

(Isaiah 61:1-2)

These two concepts, vengeance and favour, are difficult; they sound mutually exclusive, like oil and water, and yet in reality they are like two sides of the same coin. God is both holy and merciful, he is both grace and truth at the same time. The future promise of a day of vengeance and favour are both true. Yet the favour of God is by far the desire of God's heart. It's his favour that 'lasts a lifetime' (Psalm 30:5) and it's his favour that God desires for his world to experience more than anything (2 Peter 3:9). When it comes to the concept of judgement, most of us recoil from a God of judgement and struggle even with the notion of it, and yet paradoxically, deep down we all hope there is some form of judgement. Let me explain: if we were totally honest, we all want to believe that one day what's wrong with the world will be made right, what's been unjust and unfair will be made just and fair for us personally, for our families and loved ones, for our communities, for our nations and for our world.

Isaiah 61 reminds us of what Jesus came to bring to the earth: good news, both physically and spiritually, comfort for the grieving and broken-hearted, 'freedom for the captives', whether it be from addiction, fear, anxiety or any other kind of life-controlling and life-shaping restriction. The good news, the *euangelion* of God has arrived in Jesus, and now we get to carry that gospel message as the Church; we are now the good news carriers of God on earth, the ones called, equipped and empowered to continue the greater story of God. Please note, it isn't good advice or good ideas, it's good news, the greatest news!

Within this idea of waiting for the new heaven and new earth, Isaiah would caution us about something I sense is all too pervasive at times and something we need to guard against, and that's passivity. We can adopt a 'hold on till Jesus comes again' kind of approach, when Isaiah would urge us to fight that passivity and be active in our faith. These encouragements and cautions emerge in these final chapters:

> Oh, that you would rend the heavens and come down,
> that the mountains would tremble before you! . . .
> For when you did awesome things that we did not expect,
> you came down, and the mountains trembled before you.
> Since ancient times no one has heard,
> no ear has perceived,
> no eye has seen any God besides you,
> who acts on behalf of those who wait for him.
>
> (Isaiah 64:1,3-4)

In Isaiah's mind, the new heaven and new earth is not something we passively wait for, but something that we actively pursue. In the previous chapter there's a shift of focus from the declarations of what God will do to the need for the people of God to engage in that process through prayer and intercession. This culminates in chapter 64 with this cry to 'rend the heavens and come down'. The word 'rend' means to 'tear or split' – it's quite a violent action, like tearing a piece of fabric. This is powerful imagery, almost likening the heavens to a piece of clothing, a garment that could and even should be torn open so heaven can invade earth. Would that we find this kind of tenacity and urgency in our day that God would tear open the heavens, and some of heaven would come to earth.

Then we come towards the end of the story, and it's an ending that is both unexpected and at the same time predictable. Isaiah begins to describe the new heaven and the new earth:

'See, I will create
new heavens and a new earth.
The former things will not be remembered,
nor will they come to mind.
But be glad and rejoice for ever
in what I will create,
for I will create Jerusalem to be a delight
and its people a joy.
I will rejoice over Jerusalem
and take delight in my people;
the sound of weeping and of crying
will be heard in it no more.

'Never again will there be in it
an infant who lives but a few days,
or an old man who does not live out his years;
the one who dies at a hundred
will be thought a mere child;
the one who fails to reach a hundred
will be considered accursed.
They will build houses and dwell in them;
they will plant vineyards and eat their fruit.
No longer will they build houses and others live in them,
or plant and others eat.
For as the days of a tree,
so will be the days of my people;
my chosen ones will long enjoy
the work of their hands.
They will not labour in vain,
nor will they bear children doomed to misfortune;
for they will be a people blessed by the LORD,
they and their descendants with them.
Before they call I will answer;
while they are still speaking I will hear.

The wolf and the lamb will feed together,
and the lion will eat straw like the ox,
and dust will be the serpent's food.
They will neither harm nor destroy
on all my holy mountain,'
says the LORD.

(Isaiah 65:17-25)

How do we even begin to describe what heaven will be like?
Whether we are envisaging the place we go when we die,
or what the new heaven and earth will be like when Jesus
comes again, how do we even begin to describe eternity?
I love the way children try to describe heaven; in fact,
something I heard recently really amused me. A child was
being interviewed about their faith and was asked if they
loved Jesus. The child replied that they did. And then they
were asked where they were going one day. The child looked
a little bemused then excitedly shouted out the name of a
well-known theme park. Not quite the answer the interviewer
was expecting but maybe closer to the actual experience than
we might imagine.

Some of the most beautiful words in all of Scripture describe
the ending of not only our story, but of what eternity will be
like. John Watts in his commentary on Isaiah helpfully shows us
a contrast between the world we currently experience and the
new world we will get to enjoy for eternity.[75]

'Not any more'	'But'
Crying, distress	Rejoicing
An infant dying a few days old	A child living to be a hundred
An elderly person dying prematurely	One hundred deemed an early age to die
Build and another live there	Build houses and live in them
Plant for another to eat	Plant vineyards and eat their fruit
Work for nothing	Be like a tree
(Build houses for others to take)	Build for their children to live in
(Receive answers to prayer)	Before they call, God answers
(Constant violence)	Not harm or destroy in all God's mountain

Isaiah describes the new heaven in these kinds of terms:

It will be a world of joy that emanates from God himself (65:18-19);

It will be a world of safety in which illness has been eradicated (65:20);

It will be a world of abundance in which people will enjoy what they've worked for (65:21-23);

It will be a world of divine assistance in which prayers are answered before they are even uttered (65:24);

It will be a world of peace throughout the whole of creation (65:25).

Isaiah loves to call this future place 'new', but new can mean lots of things. New can mean something that never existed before, unknown, if you like, but new can also mean a new version of something all too familiar. We get a new iPhone (other brands are available!) and whereas it may be new, it's not unknown and very soon it's going to become . . . old.

New can also mean something very different from what's existed before, but new can also mean fresh, pure, young, sharp, bright. The word Isaiah uses for 'new' is the Hebrew word *chadash*, which while meaning 'new' also carries with it the idea of 'renew'. There's a sense in which it has existed before in some form and now will be returning to that form, even though it will appear brand-new and fresh. Peter describes it this way in one of his letters: 'But in keeping with his promise we are looking forward to a new heaven and a new earth, where righteousness dwells' (2 Peter 3:13).

John describes it most vividly of all in his revelation which he received on the island of Patmos: 'Then I saw "a new heaven and a new earth," for the first heaven and the first earth had passed away, and there was no longer any sea' (Revelation 21:1).

What John saw in glorious Technicolor Isaiah also glimpsed, and it was an awe-inspiring view into the end of the story. What began in a garden now ends up in a city. This is a bone of contention in our house as my wife loves gardens and the countryside and I love cities. I love the skylines, the hustle, the bustle, the energy, I love the diversity, the technology, the innovation, the architecture, I love to see what humanity can create when they collaborate together. She loves the quiet, the green, the wildlife, the fresh air, the solitude. Yet before I get too smug with my wife, the heavenly city will also be a garden city. There will be the river of life, there will be the tree of life, once accessible only to the first humans, now accessible to all.

Cities symbolise people living together, learning to co-create, learning to partner and innovate, learning to harness the uniqueness of one another for the greater good. It's also true that in the Bible cities can symbolise places of darkness and destruction, such as Babylon, but this is also true of gardens. In fact, it was in a garden that Jesus was betrayed, and yet in that garden, God's steps towards humanity's redemption were being worked out as he was moving towards his end goal of a new garden city, a new heaven and a new earth.

The heavenly city John sees in his revelation has four sides with three gates, possibly representing 'the twelve tribes of Israel' (Revelation 21:12-13). It also had 'twelve foundations', possibly a reference to the twelve apostles (Revelation 21:14), and yet the twist here is there is no reference to a temple. Could this be because in the new heaven and new earth there will be no need for a temple, as the presence of God and the Lamb is now with his people once again (Revelation 21:22)? In the end of the story, John reminds us that what was once forbidden (the fruit) is now open to all, and the leaves of the trees are now for the 'healing of the nations' and that includes all of our wounds, all of our pain, all of our sickness, all of our injustices, all of our disappointments (Revelation 22:2).

The Jerusalem Isaiah, John and other biblical writers see is not to be mistaken for the city we see today and that is so prevalent on our news feeds. The new Jerusalem is something way bigger, broader and beyond the city we see now. The apostle Paul references this when he writes to the church in Galatia, referring to 'the Jerusalem that is above' (Galatians 4:26).

The end of the story of God that will be both unexpected and predictable will sound a lot like the story sounded right in the beginning. A world at peace with itself, creation at peace with itself, humankind at peace with itself and with their God; it sounds like heaven on earth. The challenge for us is twofold.

Firstly, we need to make sure we will be there, and that is only guaranteed by our surrender to the rule and reign of Jesus in this life on this side of eternity. He will not force us into his new heaven, and he doesn't of himself condemn anyone to an eternity without him. Who we choose to walk with in this life determines who we get to walk with in the next life; that's our choice and that can happen at any moment and at any time. The thought of us choosing not to be with God for eternity breaks his heart, but that's our choice and that's what love does, it allows for the possibility of pain to the heart of the lover.

Secondly, let's give our lives to the epic adventure of helping others join us in the new heaven. At the church I get the privilege of leading, we say it this way: 'We exist to help people find and follow Jesus.' I cannot think of a better story to give my life to than that. Every time I watch people get baptised, it's like a little bit of heaven has come to earth. Every time a life is helped, a wrong is righted, an injustice made just, a brokenness made whole, a marriage restored, a young person in the care system finding their forever home, a child sponsored and lifted out of poverty . . . the list goes on and on. We get to play our part in God's epic adventure story that is heading towards an end that is both unexpected and predictable, a new heaven and earth; there is no greater story.

So now let's see how this works out in real lives. Let's head again to the living room.

The
Living Room

CHAPTER TWELVE

Greater Than Our Plans

'I say this because I know what I am planning for you,' says the LORD. 'I have good plans for you, not plans to hurt you. I will give you hope and a good future.

(Jeremiah 29:11, NCV)

The one supreme business of life is to find God's plan for your life and live it.

(E. Stanley Jones)[76]

What did you want to be when you were a kid? What were your hopes and dreams, what plans did you have? I love these suggestions from some children:

Sally, aged six: 'When I grow up I want to be a customer in a shop. I would buy broccoli, carrots and tomatoes then go home and make soup.' (A very organised domestic princess of a young lady!)

Lucas, aged five: 'When I grow up I'm going to work with rocks. For example, I'm going to throw them in the water so it makes a massive splash!' (Not quite the geologist, then!)

Maybe my favourite:

What are the three things you want to do in the future?

1. Get a girlfriend
2. Kiss her
3. Save the world![77]

There are moments in all of our lives when we realise we do have plans, goals, dreams, hopes, longings, desires, call them what you will. There came a powerful realisation of this in Isaiah's life when all that crystallised into one moment. It was a moment of unusual clarity and we talked about it right at the start of this book. The event was at his greatest moment of personal despair and confusion; his king had just died, the story that made sense of his life seemed to die with him. Then he saw the Lord, he saw someone 'greater' and in that moment all of his plans, goals, dreams, hopes, longings, desires all fell away and he was left with one overriding plan for his life . . . surrender.

Surrender to a God who is greater . . . surrender to a story that is better

For Isaiah, it happened in this moment of revelation and encounter with the glorious presence of God. I have to say that doesn't happen to me that often! When I think back on my life and story, there have been some moments of surrender that have been anything but glorious! Moments in dusty old church halls, moments in huts and shacks in Africa and India. These moments and many more were where I came face to face with the battle between my plans and a God who is greater, and here's the truth . . .

God has greater plans for your life than you do

When I say this, that doesn't mean the things we all instinctively think of – wealth, fame, power, success and millions of followers on social media. So, what does it mean, and how do we live out this life of surrender to a God who is greater than our plans? Let's look at another story that starts with a young man going about his everyday job. His view is not as glorious as Isaiah's was; in fact, he spends all day every day staring at the backside of a cow (actually an ox!). We read the story in 1 Kings 19:

> So Elijah went from there and found Elisha son of Shaphat. He was ploughing with twelve yoke of oxen, and he himself was driving the twelfth pair. Elijah went up to him and threw his cloak around him. Elisha then left his oxen and ran after Elijah. 'Let me kiss my father and mother goodbye,' he said, 'and then I will come with you.' 'Go back,' Elijah replied. 'What have I done to you?' So Elisha left him and went back. He took his yoke of oxen and slaughtered them. He burned the ploughing equipment to cook the meat and gave it to the people, and they ate. Then he set out to follow Elijah and became his servant.
>
> (1 Kings 19:19-21)

Elisha was a hardworking farmer, and there's nothing wrong with tha; hard work is a good thing. Elisha had twelve oxen, so he came from a wealthy family; in fact, his hands were full and his future was secure, so it was all good, but that doesn't mean it was all great. His job was safe, predictable, monotonous, routine, again nothing wrong with that. Could it also be true that his view of life had become safe, predictable, monotonous and routine? His view every day never changed – the backside of an ox!

Then this guy called Elijah comes along. He was a prophet; in fact, a rock star of a prophet, a veritable man of God. Elijah throws his cloak around Elisha, which while seemingly a little bit of an odd thing to do was actually extremely significant. In this culture and time, this was a symbol of calling and authority. It was Elijah inviting Elisha into a new story for his life, a story connected to the greater story of God.

On an ordinary day, God called Elisha to let go of his plans and take hold of God's plans, which are always greater. Elisha responds, as did Isaiah, decisively; he takes radical action and goes to his family, not to ask for permission but to say goodbye. He kills the oxen, burns the plough, has an awesome barbecue and then leaves.

What does all this rather strange ancient story have to do with you, me and the epic adventure of God's greater story? Let me state it again: *God has greater plans for your life than you do.*

One of the big arguments people have towards faith is that it appears 'closed-minded'. Yet the centre of the Christian faith is the assumption there is more to life than what you can see, touch, measure, taste or hear. Those who oppose this view insist that this is all there is; only what we can see, touch and observe is real, that there is nothing else. Which perspective is more closed-minded and which is more open-minded?

George Bernard Shaw famously said, 'Those who cannot change their minds cannot change anything.'[78]

After all, minds are like parachutes: they only function properly when open!

What if God has something more for you? Does it mean like Elisha you should leave your job and become a travelling prophet? Maybe, but probably not. What if instead God wants your view of life to change, to expand, to open up? What if God wants you to believe that there is more for you than your current experience of God? That he has greater plans for your life than you do? What if the story you have for your life is to fit within a greater story that God has for your life?

So, in light of this possibility, let me suggest some shifts we could make in order to posture ourselves for the greater plans God has for us.

Let's move from 'self-centred' thinking to 'others-centred' thinking

I read recently an amazing story of an Australian called James Harrison who, despite an aversion to needles, donated his blood for sixty years. His blood contained a rare antibody used to make life-saving interventions for unborn babies. He donated blood more than 1,000 times and it's thought that his blood has been instrumental in saving the lives of more than 2 million unborn babies. His story began when he was fourteen and someone else's blood helped save his life as he underwent major chest surgery.[79] I can't helping thinking of the verse, 'Freely you have received; freely give' (Matthew 10:8).

Let's move from 'here and now' to 'forever' thinking

The now famous but possibly anecdotal survey of over-ninety-five-year-olds, which asked people what they would do differently if they had their time again, was so revealing.[80] They said they'd take more risks, enjoy the small things and do something that lives on beyond themselves. That's 'greater than' thinking, that's 'forever' thinking. It was part of the core message of Jesus, who constantly encouraged people to store up treasures where it mattered the most (Matthew 6:19-20), and that's not under your bed, in your bank account, or around your house. Nobody at your funeral talks about your stuff; they only talk about your life, your impact, the difference you made and that will live on.

Let's move from 'making a living' to 'living a life' thinking

How many of us at the end of our lives might say, 'I had a nice conservatory' or 'I kept a really nice garden'? Please hear me, there's nothing wrong with either of those – by the way, my wife wishes I could do anything of worth in the garden – but surely there's more to life? We each get one shot at this thing called life; let's not settle for 'less than' but let's go for 'greater than'. If we are to do this, we have to be willing to do what Elisha did . . .

We have to be willing to burn the plough

Why burn the plough? Why not put it in the shed, why not put it on eBay or Marketplace? Why burn it? Elisha knew that as long as there was an easy way back to the old life, he would be tempted to take it. When his new life got tough, when criticism came, it would be so easy to go back to the old safe, familiar ways. In much the same way for us, to fully live in the new plans God has for us, we have to say goodbye to the old ones.

For me, I could take you to the seat in a church in the USA where God called me to give my life to the vision to build a church unchurched people would want to engage with. It's not been an easy journey; there have been many times I've been tempted to go back to a church for insiders, where we get to sing what we want to sing and do what we want to do.

Several years ago, someone left our church and, as they left, said some things I found both critical and hurtful. I'd heard it all before, to be honest: the music was too loud, the lights too bright, we were only interested in reaching young people and unchurched people, etc. It hurt but I consoled myself with the fact that this person would find another church, and we would continue to reach people that the Church wasn't reaching. Then one day the person turned up again. They came up to me at the end of the service and said some really encouraging words about what we were doing as a church. I remember that moment often, because it reminds me of the decision I made many years ago to burn the plough, and when it's hard or messy, I don't want to be tempted to go back but to press on with what God has given me and what he has called us as a church community to give our lives to, a vision that is greater than our plans. Burn the plough. There's no turning back when God calls you to something greater – it will require total surrender. Surrender always sounds so negative but actually it's not . . . but it is hard.

In the film *A League of Their Own,* Tom Hanks plays the manager of a baseball team trying to get his star pitcher to not quit. All she can keep saying is how hard it is, to which he replies profoundly that it's supposed to be hard, that's what makes it good.[81] When it comes to surrender to God, it's better than good; it's great! I'm not entirely sure you're convinced; in fact, I can almost sense some of you saying, 'Surrender is great . . . really?' Maybe what's being surfaced is what lurks beneath the surface for all of us, the real issue . . . *control.* Why we struggle to surrender, to hand over the keys, to burn the plough, often it's the issue of control. Let's head to another story, this time in the New Testament.

There was a guy in the Bible known collectively across three of the Gospel accounts for three things – he was rich, young and powerful. I mean, he had it all, right? What everyone dreams of: wealth, youth and power. Who wouldn't want to be him? Yet he knew he didn't have it all, and he came to Jesus one day and asked for something greater for his life. When we meet him in Mark 10:17 there's a strange thing going on – he is running: 'As Jesus started on his way, a man ran up to him and fell on his knees before him. "Good teacher," he asked, "what must I do to inherit eternal life?"' Important people didn't run – they still don't! Can you imagine King Charles III, Vladimir Putin, Elon Musk, Taylor Swift running down the street?

This man is paying honour to Jesus. He says 'Good teacher' – there's no other record of anyone anywhere in the rest of the Bible using this term and you'd expect Jesus to be flattered, but he's not: 'Why do you call me good? No one is good – except God alone' (v. 18).

What's going on here? Here's a man who has it all but knows there's something more; he senses there is something 'greater than'. How does Jesus respond? He makes it tough; he doesn't want this guy swept along by a tide of emotion. So, Jesus links goodness to keeping the commandments, but this guy has all of this covered, he can check every one off on the list. Then comes the real drama in the story:

> Jesus looked at him and loved him. 'One thing you lack,' he said. 'Go, sell everything you have and give to the poor, and you will have treasure in heaven. Then come, follow me.' At this the man's face fell. He went away sad, because he had great wealth.
>
> (Mark 10:21-22)

'Jesus looked at him and loved him.' He loved his energy, his passion for life. He loved what could happen with him if he surrendered to God fully. But here's the thing – what this man is really known for now all these years later isn't his wealth, youth or power; he is known for being the one who turned his back on Jesus. Does this mean if someone is rich, they need to give up their wealth? Not necessarily; after all, Jesus didn't say this to other rich people. The issue is not the wealth; the issue is what we can't give up in order to fully surrender to God. For this man it was his wealth, for others it might be their fame, their comfort, their relationships, their past, their hurt, their fear. It could be that hobby, that addiction, that need for approval, that insistence on doing things your own way, and the list goes on.

The issue is not the wealth; the issue is the control – what we can't give up

I picture the face of Jesus as this young man walks away. Jesus didn't chase after him, but his heart went out to him and then I ask, 'How many times in my life have I been this man? How many times has Jesus looked at me sad when I chose my own way over his way, my own plans over his plans?' and when I think of that, I want to commit to a new way of living where I commit every day to choosing his plans over my plans, why? He is greater than my plans and his story is a greater story. Can you imagine standing before Jesus one day and him saying to you with love in his eyes, 'I had so much more for you, but you would never let go and open your hands to receive it?'

- What's your one thing, what's your plough?
- What's your plan that's stopping you from God's greater plan?

A prayer for when our plans stand in the way of God's greater plans

Father, help me each day to open my hands to you and surrender what's in them.

Help me to be willing to embrace the plans you have for me.
Where I have planned my life and asked you to bless it, forgive me, and instead I choose to follow you and your plans for my life.

Give me the courage to let go of what is not your best plan for me, and instead take hold of what you have for me which will always be 'greater'.

Amen

CHAPTER THIRTEEN

Greater Than Our Hopes

But those who hope in the Lord
will renew their strength.

(Isaiah 40:31)

Hope is being able to see that there is light despite all
of the darkness.

(Bishop Desmond Tutu)[82]

I was feeling really good about life, faith and even myself. I was
flying home from an amazing week in Bulgaria where we had
seen God do incredible things, people becoming Christians,
hundreds of young people encountering Jesus, and I was flying
high. Until I got to Charles De Gaulle Airport in Paris, where I
was waiting for my connecting flight home to Birmingham. I
had travelled back on my own this time and needed to use the
toilet. All was good because I had plenty of time, so into said
toilet I went. I duly proceeded into the cubicle where I locked
the door and, to my horror, the handle fell off on the other
side of the door and I was locked in. 'No problem,' I thought.
'It's one of the busiest airports in the world. I will be fine. If
I can't get out, someone is bound to come in soon.' So I did

what nature needed me to do and then I waited . . . and waited . . . and waited . . . and nobody entered the men's toilets! 'Has something happened?' I thought. Had the rapture happened and I'd been left behind there in the men's toilets in Paris airport? Now I had to take action, and so I channelled my inner Bruce Willis and tried to break out of the toilet. It was not as easy as Hollywood makes it look! 'No problem,' I thought. 'There's a gap above the door, I will climb out.' So I began climbing out, my head went over no problem, my shoulders and chest went over no problem, but then came my stomach. I used to weigh a few pounds more than I do now and when I got to my stomach, I got stuck. I couldn't get over and I couldn't go back. Now I was hanging over the toilet cubicle door. Still nobody came into the men's toilet and my hope was fading fast. So, I reached into my pocket for my phone and for some reason I can't explain even now, I phoned home. Our boys were younger and my mum was babysitting.

'Mum, it's me,' I said.

'Leon, aren't you overseas?' she said.

'Yes, but I'm stuck in a toilet in Paris airport.'

To which she said, 'Leon, you're always messing about!' and she hung up on me!

As my hope was now beginning to disappear, I looked up and saw a guy walk into the toilet. 'I'm saved!' I thought and so I tried my best French on him, only to realise he was a Brummie (from Birmingham). 'Yow OK, mate? Yow stuck in the toilet?' he said in a very Brummie accent. Needless to say, he set me free and I lived to tell the tale.

There are times in all of our stories when we get stuck and hope seems to fade fast. We find ourselves in the middle, not knowing how the end will work out. There are moments when whatever we try to do to affect the story, it doesn't produce anything meaningful, and then we realise that hope is what sustains us and hope is what keeps us going until the moment when the story changes and then we can look back on that situation, now with a story to tell. When you can't see the end, hope is what keeps you going.

How important is hope? The author Hal Lindsey famously suggested we can live without food, water and air for certain amounts of time, but only a second without hope.[83] Hope for many of us is reduced to almost wishful thinking; we hope it doesn't rain today, we hope our team do well this season, we hope the worship band don't play that song again! But hope according to the greater story of God is way more than wishful thinking; in fact, biblical hope could be defined as ...

A confident expectation in the goodness of God

During the times of Isaiah, Israel experienced so much that threatened their hold on hope. While in exile, the book of Lamentations was written by the prophet Jeremiah. As he was seeing Jerusalem crumble around him, as the nation was gripped by fear, uncertainty and anxiety, he boldly called the people to hope, expressing it in these powerful words:

> The thought of my suffering and homelessness is bitter beyond words.
> I will never forget this awful time, as I grieve over my loss.
> *Yet I still dare to hope* when I remember this:
> The faithful love of the LORD never ends!
> His mercies never cease.
> Great is his faithfulness;
> his mercies begin afresh each morning.
>
> (Lamentations 3:19-23, NLT, emphasis mine)

I love that phrase, 'yet I still dare to hope'. Do you remember being dared when you were a kid? Being urged to knock on a door and run, being challenged to that extra bit of bravery or stupidity: 'Go on, then, I dare you!' I remember as a young teenager being at my friend's house. My parents were also coming over to his house, where his parents were laying on an epic spread of food for both families. For some reason, my friend dared me to add my culinary skills to the banquet and so I obliged. The cream on the trifle was replaced with salad cream, the sandwiches were given extra doses of chilli and vinegar, mustard was liberally applied; we basically murdered the meal. Then we had the brains to at least hide – well, I did anyway. I jumped into the boot of my dad's Ford Granada, then my friend decided to jump in alongside and closed the boot. Now we were both locked in the boot and soon found and forced to eat the food we had so thoughtlessly made inedible. Being dared can have some unpleasant and painful consequences.

Yet in the Bible the word 'dare' is often the word *tolmao*, which means 'to venture or to dare'. It is not so much a challenge but a call; a call to courage. It's the idea of drawing something out of us that is good, noble and purposeful. Here's the thing: if God is so much greater, this should give us the courage to hope or maybe even to hope again. Can we dare to hope?

As we begin to bring this idea of the greater story of God to a close, hope is not a bad place to leave it. We've already said that everyone has a story, that nobody gets the story they really want. We've spoken about how God redeems our story and that ultimately our story only makes sense, has meaning and purpose when it's part of his story, the greater story of God. That can sound great in theory, but what about in reality, what about in real life?

I've talked about our youngest son, Simeon. When he was around two, he was finally diagnosed with a host of complex and challenging issues, including learning disabilities, ASD, ADHD and later in life, epilepsy. As young parents who were also trying to lead a church, we were told the devastating news that Simeon would never be able to lead an independent life. I can still remember as we both sat in our car outside the hospital in tears; we were shattered by this breaking news, our hope seriously challenged for the first time in our lives.

As Simeon grew, we began to grasp what life would be like, and it certainly wasn't what we had hoped for. It wasn't in the plan; it wasn't the script we expected for our lives, or for our family. Simeon couldn't keep himself safe; he still can't. He finds it difficult to manage his emotions, regularly self-harming and hurting himself. Yet he is also a kind and compassionate young man who for someone with his particular challenges can display empathy in ways he really shouldn't be able to do. At the age of fifteen, life became so difficult for us all that we made the biggest and most painful decision of our lives, which was for Simeon to go into residential care. Life has not worked out the way we had hoped, in so many ways; we didn't get the story we wanted. We have never been able to spend time with other families, as people seem to be able to do. We never slept through the night for the first fifteen years while Simeon was at home, which can still affect our sleep patterns to this day.

In many ways, we identify with the anecdotal old story[84] where you book a holiday to Italy and while on the plane realise you aren't going to Italy, but instead you are going to Holland. You are frustrated as Italy is where the food, culture and, weather is amazing, and all your friends have been there and no disrespect to Holland, but clogs, tulips and windmills, really? Then the story makes this point. After the disappointment of realising you are not going where you had hoped you were going, you begin to discover Holland, while not Italy, has beauty all of its own to appreciate and admire. This illustration of course falls short because it's just about a holiday, not about a life, and that is so much more challenging, as we know so well. As we've said many times already – *everyone has a story, and nobody gets the story they really want.*

There have been times and are still times when sadness overwhelms us both, where at times we 'talk' to God about how we feel, and times when grief at what could have been or should have been is overwhelming. I've referred to it as a soundtrack of grief that sits underneath our lives; often, we hardly hear it but it's always there and at times it is all we can hear. *Yet I still dare to hope because God is greater than our hopes.*

Everyone has a story, nobody gets the story they want, but all of our stories can be redeemed, and ultimately our stories find sense and meaning as part of God's greater story.

How is this playing out in our story?

We've found hope in our community of faith

When Simeon was young, people in the church came around us and loved us. Several of them set up a provision for him on Sundays so we could both lead and be a part of the church community. (By the way, if you are in children's ministry in your church, and especially if you look after children with additional needs, thank you. As a parent I can tell you, it's literally a soul- and a life-saver – not only for the children, but for the families.) However resilient you may or may not be, faith was never meant to be a solitary pursuit. The story of Daniel and his three friends always inspires me. Those young men endured, and when literally thrown into a blazing furnace,

Shadrach, Meshach and Abednego encouraged one another and discovered the truth that our faith needs friends (Daniel 3). Someone once said, 'Show me your friends and I will show you your future.'[85]

We've found hope in what our story has done in us

The apostle Paul expresses it this way: 'For our light and momentary troubles are achieving for us an eternal glory that far outweighs them all' (2 Corinthians 4:17).

By the way, when Paul references 'light and momentary troubles', he is referring to being shipwrecked, stoned, flogged and put in prison (2 Corinthians 11:23-29)! Perspective is everything, isn't it?

Paul likens a weight of sufferings against a weight of glory (2 Corinthians 4:17); they may seem to weigh the same, but the value is different. Here's a question for you. What weighs more, 50kg of gold or 50kg of dirt? The same, right? But which would you rather have? The gold! The weight is the same, but the value is so different. The weight of suffering produces a weight of glory within us; that's our hope. Simeon has taught us so much about ourselves, about life, about faith and about hope. Our other son, Josh, is a children's nurse who is amazing with children with complex needs. Our church has an incredible heart for children, young people and families with additional needs, as well as many families who adopt and foster. We both feel we are more empathic as people and leaders because of our lived experience. We all walk with a limp, don't we (see Genesis 32:22-32)?

We've found hope in the promise of heaven

Have you noticed that there's only one thing we don't want to talk about as a culture these days? It used to be sex, money and politics, but we can talk about those things freely now. Death is still the subject nobody wants to talk about, and yet is the subject that puts us all on the same ground. At the time of the First World War, it was common for the average teenager to have seen several dead bodies, but nowadays it's not uncommon to reach the age of fifty and never to have seen a dead person. When it comes to death, we are unfamiliar and we are also awkward. I remember doing a funeral service some years ago and helping an older gentleman set his TomTom satnav with the directions to the crematorium (that was when you brought your satnav with you in your pocket!). As the service began, I noticed he wasn't there but then a few minutes into it, he came through the door and sat down looking a little flustered. I paused to pray and at that moment his TomTom went off in his pocket with these words: 'You have reached your final destination!'

The reality is death is the one experience we all fear, yet we will all face.

This is where hope finds its home

God is greater than our hopes and because of that, we can hope. It's our hope in heaven that helps us makes some kind of sense of our story with Simeon. How?

There will come a day when Simeon's frustrations and difficulties will be made new, not just upgraded, but brand new. There will be a day when the pangs of grief and the tears of sadness will be wiped from every eye, including ours and including yours. There will be a day when we will finally have a conversation with Simeon that we've never been able to have here on earth, and if that doesn't happen, it won't matter anyway because we will be home. The ancient words of Thomas Moore that we often hold onto are true for us as they are also true for you, 'Earth has no sorrow that heaven cannot heal'.[86]

Finally, a story from our own family that will always stay in my mind as a powerful reminder of the greater story of God we have all been invited into. It was March 2020, and my mum lay dying of cancer in a local hospice. The pandemic was just around the corner; fortunately, she missed all of that, for which we were and are very grateful. My mum was a spiritual lady; she was an inspiration to me and to so many others. She taught me so much about the greater story of God. As she was admitted to the hospice, she took in with her lots of small wooden crosses, and she gave them to everyone and anyone who came into her room. Whether it was family who didn't know Jesus, doctors, nurses or friends, they all got one and with it a message about this story of God and how it could change their life, if they would only give Jesus a chance. On 1 March she died and days later, my sister and I were talking on the phone with the funeral director, who is a family friend. I asked him, 'What happened to the cross Mum was holding in her hand when she died?' He said they couldn't find it, but I asked him to look again. A few minutes later he called and said, 'You're not going to believe this, but we looked at your mum again, and noticed her fist was clenched tight. When we gently prised open her fingers, the cross was there in the palm of her hand. She died holding onto the cross.'

When we die, and we surely will, what will we be holding onto in that moment?

What you hold onto in life can determine who you hold onto in eternity, and who will hold onto you

There is no greater story than the story of God. God created the world and it was perfect, but within that perfection, he gave humankind the greatest gift he could – free will. With that ability to choose, we did just that; we chose and with that decision, we turned our back on God and that ushered into the world disconnection, dislocation, disease, darkness and so much more. But even as that was playing out, God was already working on his ending to the story, and redemption was on its way. What Jesus did by his death and resurrection enabled every one of us who put our truth and faith in him to be reconciled to God, and not only that, but to enter into the epic adventure story of a God who is reconciling the world back to himself.

Have you responded to that invitation? If you haven't, why not do that right now?

As you consider your story and how that fits into the greater story of God, don't just know the story, know the author of the story; he invites you into a relationship with him which is greater than anything you can think of or imagine.

- Where do you find yourself losing hope the most right now?
- What one thing could you do to give yourself a tighter grip on hope?

A prayer for those wanting to hold onto hope

Father, today I hear your call to dare to hope in you again.
Today I choose to not give up but to look up.
Today I choose to believe in the dark what I knew to be true in the light.
Today I choose to hold onto you, even when I can't sense you, hear you or experience you.
Today I choose hope.

Amen

The
Playground

For all the resources and links mentioned,
scan the code to visit

www.springharvest.org/resources/no-greater-story

CHAPTER FOURTEEN

The Perfecter in the Playground

We've been in the classroom looking at the *what*, we've been in the living room looking at the *so what*, now we turn to the *now what* and we head to the playground where everyone gets to play their part in the greater story.

My life

God is the Author of our story, the Redeemer and the Perfecter. He was there at the beginning, he was there in the middle and he will be there right at the end. As our story becomes part of his greater story, how do you feel about your story right now? Maybe you feel your story with God has just started; maybe you feel in that tricky middle part of the story, or maybe you feel you're at the final stages of your story.

The famous Danish philosopher Søren Kierkegaard said, 'Life can only be understood backwards, but it must be lived forwards.'[87]

With that powerful truth in mind, here's a few ideas for you to 'play' with relating to your future story.

Write a letter to your younger self

This can be extremely cathartic and helpful. Do you have wisdom now that you wish you'd had when you were younger? What would you want to say to that person? What experiences and hindsight would you share? What advice would you give your younger self?

When you've done that, read and reflect.

Now move to idea number two.

Write a letter to you from your future self

What do I mean? In the bestselling book by Steven Covey, *The 7 Habits of Highly Effective People*, Covey asks his readers to imagine their own funeral and what words they would like to be said at their funeral.[88] Let us put a twist on that and create a letter from your future self, a little bit like the Merlin Exercise, which is a tool used to create a sense of what the future could look like. Merlin (according to legend) lived his life backwards, in that he saw the future and what needed to happen to get there.

In this letter from the future, you will describe who you have become, where God has worked in your life, obstacles and challenges you've overcome, situations you've navigated and experiences you've had. Then you will say what you did or put in place in order for that future to become a reality. Let that be an inspiration to you to lean into God, who is at work bringing to 'completion' what he began in you (Philippians 1:6).

God is always inviting us to participate in his greater story, whatever our age, stage, or circumstance. Maybe for some of us, we feel we are too old, that our time has been and gone – not so! I am constantly amazed at some of the older people in our church community still serving, still playing their part in God's story, still willing to take on another challenge for God's kingdom. I would love you to check out Faith in Later Life, an amazing organisation working across the UK to help individuals and churches find ways to release the resource and potential of older adults into the mission of God.[89] We are never too young or too old to play our part in God's epic adventure story. Don't rule yourself out when God has invited you in. Use the QR code or web link in this section to explore further.

My home

Go get your family together or whoever shares your home with you and dive into these amazing ideas from Care for the Family's Kitchen Table Project. Remember, faith grows as you go![90]

As you go ... to eat

At breakfast, ask your children to think of family or friends they could encourage today.

Talk about a Bible story that involves food, and what it might have been like for them, and what you can learn from that story.

As you go ... out

When you are in the car think of something to pray for each letter of the alphabet. Names, places, circumstances – it can be anything!

See how many cross shapes you can see. This can be done in the car or out for a walk!

As you go . . . around the house

When your family or those you share your home with are doing chores, talk about how Jesus served his disciples by washing their feet.

Talk about the fruit of the Spirit when having fruit snacks.

As you go . . . to bed

Help your children have a quiet time to listen to God and see what he wants to say to them as they sleep.

Ask your children to create a special night-time prayer with you. They can memorise it to pray every night before bed.

As you go . . . to church

Explain why you do things you do, like taking communion, baptism, singing and meeting together.

Help your child form intergenerational relationships by helping them find a prayer partner.

As an additional idea, there's a great resource Care for the Family have produced – a Summer Praise Scavenger Hunt;[91] you can access that via the QR code in this section.

My church

What role does your church have in God's greater story? The Church Jesus launched, the one he builds and sustains by his Spirit, the one he is coming back for, was always meant to be a movement, and not just any movement but an outward-facing, multicultural, multi-generational, multiplying movement. When the Church turns inwards, it stops moving; when the Church focuses on small things to the exclusion of big things, it stops moving. In the book *The God Story* written by Alain Emerson and Adam Cox from the 24:7 Prayer movement, we see a helpful reminder that the Church is meant to be 'presence', a movement of God's Spirit; it's meant to be 'family', demonstrating the beauty of diversity and difference, reflecting God's original creational intent and moving towards perfection at the end of the age. It is also meant to be 'kingdom', a colony of heaven, a community that acts as a signpost of the kingdom that is to come and a demonstration of the kingdom that has arrived.[92]

As you reflect on your church and your community, ask yourself these questions:

- Where do I see our Church moving and where do I see our church stuck?

- What part can I play in our church becoming more of an outward-facing movement?

As you and your church seek to play your part in God's greater story, why not get together with others in your church and use some or all of these creative exercises to begin to stimulate your prophetic imagination, and join with God as by his Spirit he works to make 'all things new' (Revelation 21:5, NKJV).

The front-page exercise. It's five years in the future. Imagine your local newspaper has given over its front page to reporting on the amazing impact your church is having in your community. What would the headline read? What stories would they be reporting? Why not design that front page and keep it as a prayer prompt and something you can look back on in the future?

The Merlin Exercise. As already mentioned, according to legend, Merlin lived his life backwards and made choices in the present connected to what he saw happening in the future.

Describe your church and its impact in the community in three years' time.

- What did you do in order to get there?

- What did you stop doing?

- What decisions did you make?

- What were the challenges and how did you overcome them?

Prayer walk your community. As you walk and pray around your community, listen to what you sense the Spirit of Jesus is saying to you. You may want to check out a resource The Message Trust[93] has produced along these lines, again accessible via the QR code in this section.

Rewrite Revelation 21. Starting from verse 9, attempt to rewrite Revelation 21 as if it was describing your own town, village or community. Imagine you're taken on a mountaintop to look down on your community in the new heaven and earth. How would you describe it? You are not rewriting the Bible here so don't be alarmed; you are merely using your imagination to try to picture what your community might look like in the future as God moves towards perfecting the new heaven and the new earth.

For an example of this, check out an amazing piece created by a church in inner-city London via the QR code or web link that takes you to the resources.

Epilogue

So you've made it to the end of the book! Well done, but that's not the end of the story. Isaiah saw a greater vision of God in his moment of deepest despair in Isaiah 6. He had his breath taken away realising, as we have now discovered, that God is greater than our limitations, understanding, fears, pain, mess, doubts, plans and hopes. Then God called him with these words, 'Whom shall I send? And who will go for us?' (Isaiah 6:8). Notice the plural word 'us' – God is community, Father, Son and Spirit – and Isaiah responds, 'Here am I. Send me!'

The big question now is not where Isaiah was, but where are you? Ask yourself, *'Where am I?'*

Maybe you say, 'I'm too new! I'm exploring faith or new to faith.' Maybe you say, 'I'm too young!' or, 'I'm too old! My time has come and gone.' Maybe you say, 'I'm too bad!' or, 'I'm too hurt!' Maybe you say, 'I'm too fearful' or 'too comfortable' or maybe you say, 'I'm too.................' Fill in the blank.

I have news for you, great news. You may be all these things you say, but more than that, you are loved, and the one who loves you invites you and calls you into his adventure story, which is not just about what you do but who you know and who you get to become.

Having said all this, you may well close this book and that's the end of that. If you and I are to rediscover our place in God's epic adventure, it won't happen passively or by chance, we have to take a step. Isaiah writes these poignant words calling us all to not only see what God is doing, but to become a participant in that new thing:

> Forget the former things;
> do not dwell on the past.
> See, I am doing a new thing!
> Now it springs up; do you not perceive it?
> I am making a way in the wilderness
> and streams in the wasteland.

(Isaiah 43:18-19)

God is always doing a new thing, and that is not determined by what he has done before, because he is greater. This ultimately brings us hope, and hope shapes our perspective, fuels our actions and determines our course. We are invited, called, beckoned, into a history-making story, a love story between God and his creation that he also redeemed and will one day perfect and complete.

You cannot make history if you're stuck in the past, whether it's a bad past or a good past. God's story is a call to move into the new thing he is doing, and not to allow the past to define or confine us. Yet it's also true that you cannot make good history if you don't learn from the past. Isaiah seems to be suggesting here 'forget the past', but in the previous verses he reminds the people what God did in the past. The key is in understanding the word 'dwell', which most people understand to mean the place you reside or inhabit. God tells us all to visit the past, but not to live there – don't reside or inhabit. We are to learn from the past, but not to be bound by it; to draw encouragement and strength from the past, but to have the courage and hope to forge a new path forward. We walk back to the past in order to walk more courageously into the future.

So, what's your next step?

Maybe it's to say 'yes' to the one who calls you to know him.

The now famous preacher story tells of an event where a famous actor recited Psalm 23 and the crowd went wild with applause at the end. An old man asked if he could read the psalm and at the end, no applause, but not a dry eye in the place. The actor was asked why there was the difference in reaction between the two, and he replied, 'I know the psalm but he knows the shepherd.'[94] You and I can know the story but what is far greater is to know the Author. When we know the Author, we can enter the story more fully, and then that story lives on in us as we let it. Each act of love, each step of faith, each word of encouragement, each moment of courage weaves us deeper into his story. We are invited into the ongoing work of redemption, healing and renewal, not only for ourselves, our families, our churches, our communities, but for our nations and ultimately our planet.

We are not in this story alone; we are part of a movement of God's people that stretches back in time, stretches around the world and stretches forward into eternity. So, take a step ... today.

We all have a story and all our stories matter. Very few of us get the story we really want, but all of our stories can be redeemed, find meaning and purpose when they become part of God's story. After all there is ... *no greater story.*

End Notes

Prologue

1. A.W. Tozer, *The Knowledge of the Holy* (NY: Harper & Row, 1961), p. 1.
2. J.B. Phillips, *Your God is Too Small* (London: Epworth Press, 1952).
3. John Young, *Our God is Still Too Small* (London: Hodder & Stoughton, 1988).

Introduction

4. Pope Francis, from his address to the fifth national convention of the Italian church in Florence, 10 November 2015.
5. World Health Organization fact sheets and scientific briefs from 2019 and beyond.
6. Barna research released on April 2022 featured in *Baptist News Global* and *The Christian Post*, www.barna.com/research/pastors-quitting-ministry/ (accessed 27.11.24).
7. Christopher Hitchens, *God is Not Great: How Religion Poisons Everything* (New York: Twelve Books, 2007).
8. Richard Dawkins, *The God Delusion* (New York: Bantam Press, 2006).
9. Atheist Bus Campaign, British Humanist Society and inspired by writer Ariane Sherine, 2008.
10. Source unknown.

11. Idea of three sections to Isaiah first proposed by Berhard Duhm in 1892 but suggested by several other biblical scholars. A commentary on Duhm's work can be found in an article written by Edward J. Young and found on www.galaxie.com/article/wtj10-01-02 (accessed 3.12.24).

Isaiah's AHA Moment

12. Kyle Idleman, *AHA: The God Moment That Changes Everything* (Colorado Springs, CO: David C. Cook, 2014).

13. This idea was a classic thought for many of the early Church fathers and mothers. Notably Origen in *On First Principles* and *Commentary on the Song of Songs* and St Gregory of Nyssa in *The Life of Moses* and St John of the Cross in *The Dark Night of the Soul.*

14. Attributed to G.K. Chesterton (1874–1936), English author.

PART ONE: Creator
The Classroom

15. Maya Angelou, *Wouldn't Take Nothing for My Journey Now* (New York: Random House, 1993).

Chapter One

16. Westminster Shorter Catechism, https://thewestminsterstandard.org/westminster-shorter-catechism/ (accessed 8.11.24).

17. Attributed to Confucius (551–479 BC), Chinese philosopher.

18. *The Lion, the Witch and the Wardrobe* by C.S. Lewis copyright © 1950 C.S. Lewis Pte. Ltd.

19. Descriptions of words in this book are taken from or based on *Strong's Concordance*. See James Strong, *Strong's Exhaustive Concordance of the Bible* (Carol Stream, IL: Hendrickson Publishers, 2009).

20. John Watts, *Word Biblical Commentary: Isaiah 34–66* (Nashville, TN: Thomas Nelson, 2006), p. 92.

21. Attributed to Voltaire (1694–1778), French writer, philosopher, satirist, historian.

22. Watts, *Word Biblical Commentary: Isaiah 34–66*, p. 94.

23. Robert Jastrow, *God and the Astronomers* (NY: W.W. Norton, 2001), p. 107.

24. Georges Lemaître (1894–1966), Belgian cosmologist and Catholic priest known as the Father of the Big Bang.

25. Francis Collins, *The Language of God* (NY: The Free Press, 2007), p.67

26. *Mere Christianity* by C.S. Lewis copyright © 1942, 1943, 1944, 1952 C.S. Lewis Pte. Ltd.

Chapter Two

27. St Anselm of Canterbury, 1033/34–1109.

28. John McEnroe, American tennis player, Wimbledon Championships 1981.

29. Dr Martin Luther King Jr, from a speech in New York City, 12 September 1962, www.ansomil.org/december-2022-message/ (accessed 27.11.24).

Chapter Three

30. Max Lucado, *Fearless: Imagine Your Life Without Fear* (Nashville, TN: Thomas Nelson, 2009), p. 30.

31. John Ortberg, *If You Want to Walk on Water You've Got to Get Out of the Boat* (Grand Rapids, MI: Zondervan, 2001).

32. Florence Nightingale, *Notes on Nursing: What It Is, and What It Is Not* (Mineola, NY: Dover Publications, 2001; first published 1859), p. 12.

Chapter Four

33. Helen Keller, *The Story of My Life* (NY: Doubleday, Page & Co., 1903), chapter 22.

34. Augustine of Hippo (St Augustine) (354–430), theologian and philosopher.

35. www.compassion.com/ (accessed 6.11.24).

Chapter Five

36. Gary Thomas, *Sacred Pathways: Discover Your Soul's Path to God* (Grand Rapids, MI: Zondervan, 1996).

37. Care for the Family, www.kitchentable.org.uk. See https://kitchentable.org.uk/wp-content/uploads/2021/07/As-you-go-....pdf (accessed 7.11.24). Edited for the purposes of this book.

38. A Rocha UK, www.arocha.org.uk (accessed 8.11.24).

39. Part of the A Rocha UK Mission Statement, https://arocha.org.uk/about-us/who-we-are/ (accessed 6.11.24).

PART TWO: Redeemer
The Classroom

40. Charles Wesley (1707–1788), 'O for a Thousand Tongues', https://hymnary.org/text/o_for_a_thousand_tongues_to_sing_my (accessed 6.11.24).

Chapter Six

41. Jewish saying. First appeared in the Talmud, compiled during the first millennium. *Schindler's List*, 1993, distributed by Universal Pictures.

42. Commonly held view of Hebrew Scripture interpretation. An example would be H.L. Stack and Günter Stemberger, *Introduction to the Talmud and Midrash* (Minneapolis, MN: Fortress Press, 1991).

43. Watts, *Word Biblical Commentary: Isaiah 1–33*, p. 104.

44. Alec Motyer, *The Prophecy of Isaiah* (Lisle, IL: IVP Academic, 1998), p. 98.

45. John Stott, *The Cross of Christ* (Downers Grove, IL: InterVarsity Press, 1986), p. 158.

46. Philip Bliss (1838–1876), 'Man of Sorrows, What a Name' www.hymnal.net/en/hymn/h/108 (accessed 6.11.24).

47. Motyer, *The Prophecy of Isaiah*, p. 500.

Chapter Seven

48. Matt Chandler, Sermon, 'The Story of the Bible', Village Church, www.thevillagechurch.net/resources/ (accessed 27.11.24).

49. Alan Deutschman, *Change or Die* (NY: Harper Collins, 2007).

50. The Johari Window, created by Jospeh Luft and Harrington Ingham in 1955.

51. Tim Keller, *The Reason for God: Belief in an Age of Skepticism* (NY: Dutton, 2008), p. 14.

52. PEACE Words and Music by Benjamin Hastings, Michael Fatkin and Melodie Wagner © 2018 Hillsong Music Publishing Australia.

Chapter Eight

53. *The Problem of Pain* by C.S. Lewis copyright © 1940 C.S. Lewis Pte. Ltd.

54. Epicurus (341 BC–270 BC), Greek philosopher.

55. R.E.M., 'Everybody Hurts' from the album *Automatic for the People* (1992), Warner Bros.

56. *Star Trek V: The Final Frontier*, 1989, distributed by Paramount Pictures.

57. Exact time and location not known.

58. Eugene Peterson, *A Long Obedience in the Same Direction* (Downers Grove, IL: InterVarsity Press, 2000), p. 159.

Chapter Nine

59. Lillian Smith, *Killers of the Dream* (NY: W.W. Norton & Company, 1994), p. 49.

60. *Surprised By Joy* by C.S. Lewis copyright © 1955 C.S. Lewis Pte. Ltd.

61. Madeleine L'Engle, *The Rock That is Higher: Story as Truth* (Wheaton, IL: Harold Shaw Publishers, 1993), p. 52.

62. Mother Teresa, ed. Brian Koloduejchuk, MC, *Come Be My Light* (NY: Doubleday Religion, 2007).

Chapter Ten

63. Mark Greenwood, www.revmarkgreenwood.com (accessed 8.11.24).

64. www.marieaitken.com/keep-it-simple (accessed 21.11.24).

65. Compassion UK, www.compassionuk.org (accessed 8.11.24).

66. Care for the Family, www.kitchentable.org. uk. See https://kitchentable.org.uk/wp-content/ uploads/2021/07/As-you-go-....pdf (accessed 7.11.24). Edited for the purposes of this book.

67. Further Faster Network, www.furtherfaster.network (accessed 8.11.24).

68. https://homeforgood.org.uk/ (accessed 7.11.24).

Chapter Eleven

69. Aristotle (384 BC–322 BC), Greek philosopher.

70. Dallas Willard, *The Divine Conspiracy: Rediscovering Our Hidden Life in God* (San Francisco, CA: HarperCollins, 1998), p. 321.

71. Tim Keller, *Hope in Times of Fear* (NY: Viking, 2021).

72. *Mastermind*, BBC first aired in 1972.

73. Motyer, *The Prophecy of Isaiah*, p. 496.

74. Gordon-Conwell Theological report 2024, https://goodfaithmedia.org/global-christian-population-projected-to-reach-3-3-billion-by-2050/ (accessed 21.11.24).

75. Watts, *Word Biblical Commentary Isaiah 34–66*, p. 354.

Chapter Twelve

76. E. Stanley Jones, *The Christ of the Indian Road* (London: Hodder & Stoughton, 1925). See www.azquotes.com/author/7566-E_Stanley_Jones (accessed 27.11.24).

77. Largely anecdotal from unknown sources. Original source unfound.

78. George Bernard Shaw, *The Doctor's Dilemma* (London: Penguin Classics, 2001), p. 61.

79. James Harrison (1936–), Australian. Known as 'the man with the golden arm', awarded the Medal of the Order of Australia on 7 June 1999. www.lifeblood.com.au/news-and-stories/stories/james-harrison (accessed 21.11.24).

80. Survey of over-ninety-five-year-olds is largely anecdotal, although referenced in many other writings and articles.

81. *A League of Their Own*, 1992, distributed by Columbia Pictures.

Chapter Thirteen

82. Bishop Desmond Tutu, *God Has a Dream: A Vision of Hope for Our Time* (NY: Doubleday, 2004), p. 14.

83. www.goodreads.com/quotes/193469-man-can-live-about-forty-days-without-food-about-three (accessed 7.11.24).

84. Source unknown.

85. Attributed to Dan Peña, (1945–), American businessman.

86. Thomas Moore (1779–1852), altered by Thomas Hastings (1784–1872), 'Come, Ye Disconsolate, Where'er Ye Languish', www.hymnal.net/en/hymn/h/684 (accessed 21.11.24).

Chapter Fourteen

87. Søren Kierkegaard, *Journals & Papers* (Bloomington, IN: Indiana University Press, 1967).

88. Stephen R. Covey, *The 7 Habits of Highly Effective People* (NY: Free Press, 1989).

89. https://faithinlaterlife.org/about-us/people/ (accessed 7.11.24).

90. Care for the Family, www.kitchentable.org. uk. See https://kitchentable.org.uk/wp-content/ uploads/2021/07/As-you-go-....pdf (accessed 7.11.24). Edited for the purposes of this book.

91. https://kitchentable.org.uk/resource/summer-praise-scavenger-hunt/ (accessed 7.11.24).

92. Alain Emerson and Adam Cox, *The God Story* (London: SPCK, 2024).

93. www.message.org.uk/ (accessed 7.11.24).

Epilogue

94. Source unfound.